Joe the Great

Joe Canning
Irish Sporting Legend

Paul O'Flynn

Gill Books

Gill Books
Hume Avenue
Park West
Dublin 12
www.gillbooks.ie

Gill Books is an imprint of M.H. Gill and Co.

© Paul O'Flynn 2025

978 07171 8583 2

Edited by Natasha Mac a'Bháird
Proofread by Liza Costello
Printed and bound in Sweden by Scandbook AB
Print origination by Padraig McCormack
This book is typeset in 12pt on 18pt, Tahoma.

For permission to reproduce artwork, the author and publisher gratefully acknowledge the following: ©iStockPhoto

The paper used in this book comes from the wood pulp of sustainably managed forests.

This book has been produced in accordance with guidelines provided by Dyslexia Ireland.

All rights reserved.
No part of this publication may be copied, reproduced or transmitted in any form or by any means, without written permission of the publishers.

To the best of our knowledge, this book complies in full with the requirements of the General Product Safety Regulation (GPSR). For further information and help with any safety queries, please contact us at productsafety@gill.ie.

A CIP catalogue record for this book is available from the British Library.

5 4 3 2 1

Author's note

This book is based on Joe Canning's life and career. It would be impossible for me to go back in time and listen in to all of the conversations with Joe that have taken place over the years, so I have had to imagine them. I also haven't actually been in the dressing rooms or Joe's home or inside his head, because that would just be weird. However, all of the scores and matches are real and all of Joe's achievements mentioned in the book are factual. He really is one of the hardest working GAA players ever.

About the author

Paul O'Flynn is an RTÉ News and Sport presenter and journalist. A graduate of DCU with a BA in Journalism and an MA in International Relations, he is also currently an associate lecturer at his alma mater. He is a keen sportsperson and amateur swimmer, and in 2018 he was the winner of the Liffey Swim. This is his fifth Irish Sporting Legends biography, following *Ireland's Call*, *Josh the Flyer*, *King Henry* and *Go, Johnny, Go!*

Joe Canning is a five-time All Star hurler. He lives in Limerick with his wife Meg and daughter Josie. He is an Ambassador for UNICEF Ireland, an organisation dedicated to protecting children's rights and ensuring access to health, education, and protection for every child. Find out more at www.unicef.ie.

Chapter 1

All-Ireland Glory

They could hear the noise from the dressing room. It was the sound of 82,300 roaring fans. It was almost time.

Joe Canning looked across to his captain David Burke and winked. At the end of the long tunnel they could see the stadium packed with the blue and white of Waterford and the maroon and white of Galway. 'Today's the day,' said Joe.

'No more near misses,' replied Burke. 'The pain of the last 29 years ends today.'

Joe the Great

They took a deep breath, pulled on their helmets and walked out onto the lush green pitch of Croke Park for the 2017 All-Ireland hurling final. The Galway fans roared at the sight of their heroes, waving their flags, banners and headbands.

Galway had been the best team all season and now they faced Waterford in the final. It was going to be tough. Waterford had Hurler of the Year Austin Gleeson and the legendary Michael 'Brick' Walsh on their side. But Galway had Joe.

Joe had been set for greatness from a young age. He had shone on Galway's minor and under-21 teams and was named Young Hurler of the Year. He was a club champion and the championship's top scorer. He was even a three-time All Star. But for all his greatness, he had never got his hands on the Liam MacCarthy Cup. Would that all end today?

This was his fourth All-Ireland final. He had already drawn one and lost two before. But Joe had a sense of calm now. Everything was going to be okay.

All-Ireland Glory

The noise in the stadium rose. The referee picked up the sliotar. Joe tightened the straps of his helmet, gripped his hurley and looked up to the heavens. This was it.

The whistle blew. Game on!

Joe sprang into action. He snatched the ball on the 45-metre line, shouldering two Waterford defenders. He twisted his body, swung his arms and let rip.

Over the bar!

Galway were out of the traps and in front after just 20 seconds.

'Come on, boys!' roared Joe.

Johnny Coen, Joseph Cooney and Cathal Mannion quickly followed, sticking over great points. It was a dream start. But Waterford soon found their feet and the back of the net. Captain Kevin Moran led by example, scoring a goal.

It was all action, tight and tense. Galway were scoring with every shot. Joe, as usual, was at the heart of the action. He scored two more points in a row.

Joe the Great

But they couldn't keep the Munster men out. Kieran Bennett scored another Waterford goal from way out on the touchline. It was a shock to the Galway defence.

Joe was fuming. 'Don't let the heads drop, lads!'

He sliced over a perfect sideline cut. It was his trademark move. He landed his first free just before half-time. A sweet strike that left Galway narrowly ahead at the break.

The dressing room was calm as Galway manager Micheál Donoghue spoke to the players. Joe took it all in. He knew the game was theirs for the taking.

'We've waited 29 years for this, lads. This is what all the training was for. Run your hearts out. Use every bit of energy you have and in 35 minutes we'll be All-Ireland champions,' he roared as he slammed his fist into the base of his hurley.

But back on the pitch, Waterford pushed ahead for the first time. Galway needed a leader now and Joe stepped up. He moved to centre-forward, striking two more frees.

All-Ireland Glory

With 20 minutes left, it was all square. It was now or never. David Burke landed two more points and Joe stuck over another free.

'You're flying today,' said Burke.

'Come on!' Joe roared to the crowd.

With a minute to go, Niall Burke was fouled and Joe stepped up for the free. He took a few deep breaths as he stood over the ball. He thought of his childhood growing up, playing with his brothers. He thought of his parents, his friends, teammates and everyone in Galway.

'Do it for them,' he thought to himself.

Joe took aim, fired and split the posts. Right through the middle.

What a score! Does he ever miss? Canning does it again!

Three minutes of stoppage time were added but Galway knew it was in the bag. The referee blew the whistle.

Galway are the All-Ireland champions!

Joe turned to face the crowd, pumping his fists in celebration. More than anything else, he felt a sense of relief, just pure emotion. They had finally done it. People young and old were crying in the stands. His mam and dad were somewhere in the crowd too. He soon found them and they shared big hugs and tears.

'Can you believe it, Mam? We did it!' said Joe.

'I'm so proud of you,' she replied as she squeezed him in tight to her.

'I couldn't have done it without you, Mam.'

Joe took his time making his way back to the dressing room. He took it all in, talking to everyone and celebrating.

Inside was wild. The lads were singing 'We Are the Champions'. David Burke was standing there in just his shorts. Johnny Glynn was roaring at the top of his voice. Gearóid McInerney, Johnny Coen and Joseph Cooney were hugging and swaying.

'This is what it's all about,' thought Joe. All the training in the cold nights of winter, all the healthy eating and the puck-abouts perfecting his skills. All those years of defeat, the criticism

All-Ireland Glory

and pain. It was all worth it now to stand in Croke Park with his best friends, teammates and brothers. Together in glory.

The celebrations went on into the night. The next day, they all went home to Galway. The Liam MacCarthy Cup crossed the banks of the River Shannon and later arrived in Portumna and Gortanumera, Joe's hometown where this amazing story all began.

Chapter 2

Seán and Josephine

Hurling was in Joe Canning's blood before he was even born. A few weeks before he arrived, Galway had won the 1988 All-Ireland championship for the second year in a row, beating Tipperary by 1-15 to 0-14. The excitement around the county had gone through the roof that summer.

Joe's dad, Seán, was worried his wife Josephine was getting carried away.

Seán and Josephine

'I hope that baby doesn't come early,' he laughed as she jumped for joy when local hero Tony Keady stuck over another point at Croke Park. The celebrations in the Canning house and around Galway were wild that afternoon. They were right to enjoy the moment. They didn't know it at the time, but it would be 29 long years before Galway won another All-Ireland. And the baby boy about to be born would be the county's new hurling hero.

Just a few weeks later, on 11 October, little Joe came into the world. A beautiful bouncing baby with blond hair and blue eyes. He was a bundle of energy and his mam and dad were full of joy.

'Isn't he beautiful?' said his mam, Josephine. 'What will we call him?'

'I don't know. I think he's your pet already,' said his dad, Seán. 'Beautiful, just like his mother. We should name him after you.'

'Josephine?!'

'Well, Joseph. Joe. He looks like a Joe,' said Seán.

Joe the Great

The little baby opened his eyes and looked up at them. His mam and dad couldn't wait to bring him home to meet his five older brothers and one sister.

Seán and Josephine were as happy as when they first met in 1964, at a dance in the Crystal Ballroom in Kiltormer, just outside Ballinasloe.

Seán was only nineteen and Josephine was two years younger than him. He saw her across the room and picked up the courage to ask her to dance. They discovered that they lived near each other and that they had both grown up on a farm. More importantly, they were both huge hurling fans. They were a perfect match.

Josephine was from a big family. When they were young they would have puck-abouts in the field beside her house. One of her brothers went on to win an All-Ireland club medal with his local team. As she grew up, all the talk in her house was about hurling.

The Cannings were already a famous hurling family. Seán and his brother Frankie

Seán and Josephine

lived for the game and always carried a hurley in their hands, even when they were out driving cattle in the evening. They had no car back then and had to cycle to all their games. Sometimes they were more than 15 kilometres away. They were often worn out before they even played the match!

At the weekend, the family would all listen to the match commentary on the radio together. There was no TV, iPhones or YouTube back then, so Seán and Frankie had to imagine the moves their heroes pulled off on the pitch.

The brothers played intermediate for Galway together. Frankie went on to line out for the seniors. But times were hard back then. There were very few jobs in County Galway, so Frankie moved to London to find work. It looked like the end of his Galway dream. In London, he worked as a builder and in bars, but he still played hurling every weekend. Over the years he won six London championships.

Frank was a tough player. He once continued playing a match against Cork, even after his two front teeth had been knocked out! The Cannings were always known as hard men on the pitch. It was something Joe would show too as he grew up.

Galway won the All-Ireland final in 1980 and Frankie felt he was missing out. All his former teammates were celebrating in Croke Park and he was hundreds of miles away in London. He decided to return home to Galway and have one more crack at an All-Ireland win. He was recalled to the panel but they came up short the next year, losing the final to Offaly by just three points. Still, he had an All-Ireland runners-up medal for his efforts and had laid the groundwork for the success of his nephew over the coming years.

When Seán and Josephine married in 1969, Josephine gave up her job as a nurse and moved to Gortanumera, just outside Portumna in south-east Galway. There wasn't much more than a crossroads in the middle of the countryside, with a small school, a church and a hurling pitch. They made their home there

Seán and Josephine

and started a family. With two great hurling clans coming together, it was no surprise that their children had a natural talent for the game. Their first son was Séamus. Next came Frank, Davy, Ollie, Ivan and a sister, Deirdre. Each one was more talented than the last. Joe came along seven years later, the best of them all.

'A gift from God,' his dad called him. In just a few short years, everyone in Galway and across Ireland would know about him. He was a gift, alright. A gift from the hurling gods.

Chapter 3

First Steps

From the moment Joe could walk it was hurling, hurling, hurling. It was his life. Before he was even two years old, he had pulled on one of his big brother's helmets and the blue and yellow jersey of the local club, Portumna. It was way too big for him and hung below his knees. He often grabbed a hurley and sliotar and ran around the house, trying to solo or strike the ball, just like his older brothers. In his head, he was already playing for Galway at Croke Park.

First Steps

The rest of the family thought it was so funny when little Joe performed his routine.

Soon Joe was out in the yard, growing, getting stronger and starting to strike the ball with ease. His family knew he was a natural. Even by the Cannings' standards, it was clear that Joe was extra special. He just needed to practise his skills. He already had the perfect team to learn from.

His oldest brother, Séamus, was 19 years older than Joe. He taught Joe to look after himself on the pitch and to stand up to bigger, stronger players. Séamus was the joker of the family and was always relaxed. He never got too uptight before games. Joe learned how to be calm from him.

Frank taught him the important lesson that talent wasn't everything.

'You have to work, Joe,' he would say. 'Even the most talented don't make it without hard work.'

Davy, the deadly corner-forward, gave Joe his eye for goal.

Joe the Great

'When you have a chance, pull the trigger. Don't wait,' he would tell Joe.

Davy also showed him the proper way to take a sideline cut. It was a skill that Joe would perfect as he grew older. But for now, Joe just watched him and took it all in.

Ivan was the goalkeeper. His brothers joked that Ivan was the lazy one and didn't like running too much, so he went in goal instead.

But Ivan was brave and fearless. He was happy to stand in front of a sliotar flying right towards him. He had a sharp eye for following the ball and he showed Joe everything he knew.

His sister Deirdre was a fine camogie player and played for Galway. She brought him to matches as he was growing up and showed him how to be confident.

'If you don't believe in yourself, Joe, nobody else will,' she would tell him. Deirdre looked out for all her brothers. If anybody ever said a bad word about the Cannings, she was the first to defend them.

First Steps

Then there was Ollie. Until Joe came along, Ollie had been the most talented of the Cannings. He was a natural born defender, as hard as nails. He was always pucking about with Joe, hooking, blocking and tackling. He showed him the tricks that defenders used and what a forward should do to escape them.

Joe's family helped him to become an all-round great hurler. Joe looked up to each of them. But at home he was just ordinary Joe, their little brother. The Cannings were a normal, close family who did most things together like eating meals around the kitchen table and watching TV. Their aunties, uncles and cousins lived close by too. They all spent a lot of time together. That's the way it was in their house. Hurling was huge but family came first.

They all knew that Joe was born with an extra special talent. Now he had to put it to use.

Joe would spend almost every minute he had outside on the lawn with a hurley and sliotar in his hands. His favourite trick was to hit the ball over the house while the family sheepdog Ross ran to fetch it. Joe would practise for hours every day until he could do it perfectly. Sometimes it made his mam cross.

'Be careful not to smash any windows,' she would shout. 'And mind the poor dog! He'll be worn out chasing after those balls!'

They often had family battles on the lawn together, on long summer nights when the sun never seemed to go down. Four-a-side games that their mam and dad would join too. Ollie usually marked Joe and treated him like any other opponent. He never went easy on him, grabbing his jersey or sliding an elbow into his ribs. Joe learned early on that he had to take the knocks and play on.

The first time Joe got the better of Ollie was a special moment. He was playing out the front of the house on the same team as his dad. His dad pucked it short to Deirdre. She looked up and saw Joe. Ollie was marking him tight.

'Right, Joe!' Deirdre shouted as she fired a low ball along the ground into space.

First Steps

Joe darted out in front of Ollie. He scooped up the ball with the hurley in one movement, as quick as lightning. He was waiting for a clatter from Ollie, so he faked to go right and then turned left. Ollie fell for it. Joe left him for dead.

'Ya boya, Joe!' roared his dad.

Joe was free now and charging down on goal. Only Ivan stood in his way. Joe looked him in the eye, set himself and blasted it right into the top corner. Ollie could only watch as it went whizzing past.

Gooooooooaaaaaaalllllll!

'Yeess!' Joe screamed as he shook his fist in the air. 'Did you like that, Ollie? I skinned you!'

Ollie wasn't one bit happy.

'Next time I'll flake you,' he said. 'I won't be going easy on you any more.'

He was disgusted Joe had beaten him but he was also secretly delighted his little brother was getting better all the time.

At night, when it was too dark to hurl or he had no energy left, Joe would sit down and watch videos of old Portumna games over and over. He loved watching his brothers in action and tried to learn how they played the game.

He would study the tactics and then ask his dad a hundred questions.

'Why did they play the ball there?'

'Who's marking the full-forward?'

'Why didn't he drill it in low?'

He was always trying to learn everything about the game.

'Come on, Joe. Bedtime.' His mam would eventually call an end to it.

'Ah, Mam! Just one more video, please? I'm not even tired,' he would beg.

'No, that's it now. You've school tomorrow.'

As his dad tucked him into bed, he always asked for one more story. 'Tell me about the time Uncle Frankie played for London against Galway, Dad,' said Joe.

His dad would then tell him one of the many wonderful tales in the history of Galway hurling.

First Steps

When Joe fell asleep, he dreamed that one day he would be the hero for Galway, scoring the winning point at Croke Park with the crowd cheering his name.

Chapter 4

Gortanumera

Joe didn't have far to travel to school. It was only a short walk to the crossroads in Gortanumera, past the church, to the tiny school with just two teachers. Damien Hayes lived across the road too. He was already a great hurler who Joe looked up to. He was a few years older than Joe but they became great friends and teammates over time.

There was some land beside his house that belonged to Joe's family. Behind that was a

Gortanumera

field with goalposts. It didn't look like much but it was the field of Joe's dreams.

There wasn't even a shop in Gortanumera, so Joe and his family spent a lot of time travelling in and out to Portumna, a big town not too far away. He loved going along for the spin. With so many brothers and a sister, there often wasn't enough room in the car for him. He would have to stay and help out at home instead. He thought it was so unfair.

Sometimes there would be a spare spot and he would head into town to watch a match. He looked on from the sidelines, taking it all in and dreaming of the day it would be his turn. He was itching to play his part. But for now he had to make do with the field in Gortanumera, where he played his first proper match.

The big day finally arrived. Joe hadn't even turned 10 years old yet, but it was time for him to play a real game. He was representing his school against another local team. He was so excited. He could barely sleep the night before.

Joe the Great

'Come on, Joe, it's bedtime,' his mam told him. 'You'll wear a hole in those boots if you polish them anymore.'

Joe wanted to look the part for his first big match. He fiddled with the straps on his helmet, making sure they were just right. He wrapped a new grip around his hurley so it felt nice and fresh. His boots were sparkling clean.

'I can't wait to get out there and play, Mam. I hope we win,' he said as he jumped into bed.

The next day the sun was shining. There wasn't much of a breeze. It was a perfect day for a game of hurling.

Joe sat at his desk in school looking out the window. All he could think about was the game. He wasn't listening to his teacher at all. Finally, the bell rang and school was over for the day. It was game time.

Joe and his friends ran across the road and jumped over the stone wall onto the pitch. They were shouting and roaring with excitement. The ground was bumpy and the grass hadn't been cut for a while. There were even a few daisies and dandelions growing in places. It didn't matter to Joe and his teammates. This was their first ever match and they badly wanted to win it.

Joe pulled on his shorts, socks and shiny boots and slipped on his jersey. Number 6. He put on his helmet and clipped the straps tight. He picked up his hurley, feeling the weight of it as he took a few practice swings across the blades of grass. It was time. The game was on and Joe was ready for action.

The referee blew the whistle and threw the ball in. Joe won the ball straight away and barged past a couple of players as if they weren't there. His tiny figure sped down the pitch. He was straight through on goal just seconds into the match. He took one look up, picked his spot and blasted a powerful shot right into the back of the net.

Goooooooaaaaaaallllll!

Joe jumped into the air with delight. It was his first ever goal in a real match.

What a feeling!

Joe the Great

A shiver ran down his spine as his teammates came over to celebrate with him. Their teacher on the sideline had to remind them not to get too carried away. After all, the game was only starting!

'Get back, lads. Joe, keep the head!' he shouted.

There was no need for their teacher to worry. Joe was on fire that day and there was no way his school was losing.

Joe remembered everything he had learned from playing with his family on the lawn at home. He hooked like Ollie. He blocked like Ivan. He ran like Deirdre and struck frees like Frank. He sliced sideline cuts like Davy and fired unstoppable shots like Séamus. He was on the end of ball after ball. Sometimes it seemed like there were no other players on the pitch.

He hit a point from the left and another from the right. He knocked over a free with ease and slipped over another one after a solo run.

Gortanumera

And the goals just kept on coming. One had a lovely, flicked finish. Another was a blaster into the top corner. He quickly scored another with a strong groundstroke. The other team's goalkeeper didn't know what was happening. The parents on the touchline were wondering who the little boy with number 6 on his back was. He was magic.

Joe was head and shoulders above all the other players on the pitch. He finished the game with a remarkable four goals and six points. The referee blew the final whistle. Joe roared with delight.

Joe's classmates crowded around him, cheering and slapping him on the back.

'There's plenty more to come,' said Joe. 'We're only getting started.'

Chapter 5
Mischief

Joe didn't mind school too much and he liked his teachers. But he always wanted to be out on the hurling pitch instead. Every day, he would sit in the classroom staring out the window, dreaming of scoring another point or goal. He would do anything he could to practise more. Wherever Joe was, he would have a hurley and sliotar in his hand. First thing in the morning. On his walk to school. Even in the classroom if the teacher didn't see

Mischief

him! Joe would always be bouncing the ball on the end of the stick.

At home he looked for every chance to practise too. He was always trying out new skills and ways to get better. Sometimes he went a bit too far!

One day, he was practising his free taking. He wanted to be more accurate, to hit the ball exactly where he wanted it to go. It was a hot summer's day. His dad and brothers had been working hard at the silage. Joe was still small but he tagged along and helped out when he could. Of course, he brought his hurley and sliotar with him.

By the evening they were finished. All the silage was gathered, wrapped in black plastic and covered with old tyres from tractors and cars. They were all thirsty and hungry from the work but delighted with a job well done.

'That's that for another year,' said his brother Ollie.

'Fair play, lads. Couldn't have done it without you,' said his dad Seán.

Joe the Great

It was time to go back to the house for tea. But Joe had other ideas.

'I'll follow you in a minute,' he said.

Joe had been eyeing up the tyres all day. 'They would be perfect for target practice,' he thought. If he could just find a bit of rope to hang them up, he could practise his frees. But he needed help.

'Pssst ... pssst ... Ollie,' he whispered. 'Come here for a second. I need a hand.'

Joe explained his plan to Ollie. They were going to take a couple of tyres from the top of the silage mound. Nobody would notice a few missing. They would roll them up to the back of the shed and hang them at different heights.

'Joe, you're a genius!' laughed Ollie. 'That's a great idea. Let's do it now while Dad's not here.'

Ollie climbed up first because he was the biggest. Joe followed him. The silage mound was really high. He had to be careful not to rip the plastic. His hands were slipping as he got near the top but, with one last pull, he

Mischief

was up. He saw three perfect tyres right at the back. One from a big tractor's back wheel, a small one from a front wheel and a car tyre. All different sizes. Just the job!

The big tractor tyre was so heavy that the two brothers needed all their strength to flip it over and shove it off the mound. They were sweating from all the effort. They gave it one last big shove.

'One, two, three. Go!'

The tyre crashed down to the ground and rolled a couple of times before coming to a stop. Joe and Ollie burst out laughing.

'Yeess!' They high-fived.

The others were much easier to shove off the mound. Ollie and Joe jumped to the ground and rolled the tyres to the back of the shed.

They found a bit of old rope and tied a loop around each of them. The next hard bit was lifting them up. Joe stood under the big tractor tyre as Ollie pulled the rope as hard as he could.

'Higher, Ollie, higher!' shouted Joe. 'Steady as she goes now.'

Joe the Great

Ollie felt like his arms were going to fall off.

'Just a little bit more, Ollie,' said Joe. 'Whoa, whoa. Perfect. That's the job.'

Ollie tied a double knot on the rope, nice and tight.

'That's not going anywhere,' he said proudly.

They did the same with the two smaller tyres. When they finished, they stood back to admire their work. The three tyres sat high along the back of the shed. A big, medium and small target, all at different heights. It was perfect.

'Nicely done, Ollie!' said Joe.

'Well, it was your idea, Joe,' laughed Ollie as he playfully punched his younger brother on the shoulder. 'Come on. We better go up for tea.'

They thought they had gotten away with it. The next day, their dad came back up from the farm.

'Anyone know anything about a few tyres going missing from the silage?' he asked.

Joe and Ollie looked at each other. They thought they had better come clean.

Mischief

'Eh, we took them, Dad. For target practice,' said Joe.

The two brothers thought they were in big trouble but their dad burst out laughing.

'That's a brilliant idea,' he said. 'Sure, let's go have a game now.'

They all went down to the shed to try out Joe's new shooting range. It was great fun.

Over the years, Joe would perfect his free-taking technique at that very wall. Driving ball after ball straight through the middle. He would take a step further back every time. His brothers practised too. Even though Joe was much smaller, he was already better than them.

'I bet you can't hit 10 in a row, Joe!' Ollie dared him.

'Watch me!' said Joe with a grin. He never missed.

Joe could sometimes go missing on long summer days. His mam and dad usually knew where to find him. Sometimes he would be down in Portumna woods, pucking a ball around or joining his friends for a dip in the River Shannon. But usually Joe would be found at the nearby workshop of Tony Keady.

Tony was a legendary Galway hurler. He was Joe's hero. He was the star of the Galway team that won the All-Ireland in 1988, the year Joe was born. His workshop was just down the road from Joe's school and Joe often called over. He wanted to learn as much as he could from him. Joe could watch him making hurleys for hours. He was always asking for more tips on how to get better.

Sometimes when Tony got home from work, he would complain that he had got nothing done because Joe Canning was down with him all day! Tony was a brilliant hurley maker. But Joe was very fussy about the way he wanted his hurley. He wanted the weight and feel of it to be just right. Sometimes Joe's mam would be waiting out in the car for ages. Joe would be inside pucking around and messing with Tony. He would lose track of time. The workshop was a magical place.

Mischief

Joe loved that Tony always had a bit of mischief about him. He always had a twinkle in his eye when he was up to something. Tony had a great deal of time for Joe. He talked him through what he was doing and showed him another new skill. Tony liked that Joe was following in his footsteps. He knew that Joe was about to become another Galway great.

Chapter 6

The Portumna Prodigy

With all the children playing so much sport, there was always plenty of washing to be done in the Canning house. The blue and yellow socks and jerseys of Portumna hung with pride on the clothesline outside.

Joe often helped to hang out the clothes to dry. Pegging the wet gear on the line, he dreamed of wearing the famous Portumna jersey, just like his brothers, uncles and dad before him.

The Portumna Prodigy

The club was part of the Canning family. When his brother Ollie made his First Holy Communion, he stood for a family photo dressed in his best suit. His dad stood beside him, togged out in Portumna gear! He had a match that afternoon. Not even his son's communion was going to stop him. That's how much the Portumna club meant to the Cannings.

Joe's primary school days were coming to an end. But before he made the big leap to secondary school, he had to play in the national school final. It was always played on the local pitch beside his school in Gortanumera. It was a seven-a-side match with small goals. Tony Keady's nephew and niece were in school with Joe, so he came along to watch them. He was asked to stand in as umpire. Joe was so excited that the legend was going to see him play. He decided to put on a show.

Joe ruled the game from start to finish. He caught high in the air. He ran skilful solos,

Joe the Great

flicking, hooking and blocking. He showed some super striking. He was on fire!

'Good man, Joe,' shouted Tony as he landed another point. Joe was delighted.

The moment of the match came in the second half. Joe's team had lost the ball so he ran back as hard as he could. He knew defending was just as important as scoring for the team. He caught up with the attacker and landed a hard shoulder.

'Play on!' said the referee. It was a fair hit and Joe was on the move.

Joe scooped to lift the ball. In one move it was up on his stick. He ran like the wind. He twisted past one, two, three defenders! They just couldn't stop him. He was in on goal now. He slowed a little and flicked the ball into his hand. Still running, he looked at the goalkeeper. In a flash, he decided to drill it low into the corner.

He let rip.

Whoosh! Gooooooooaaaaaaalllllll!

'Yeesss!' Joe let out a roar.

His teammates ran after him to celebrate.

The Portumna Prodigy

'Great stuff, Joe!' said Tony Keady. He gave Joe a thumbs up. 'Portumna will be looking for you soon!'

'It's all thanks to the fine hurley you made me, Tony!' Joe laughed back.

He was so happy. His team had won. The great Tony Keady had seen him in action. Was it really true? Could he be playing for Portumna soon?

Everyone knew the Cannings were great hurlers. Now word was spreading around the parish and beyond that Joe was a special talent. Over the next few years, he just got better and better. People were starting to sit up and take notice. Joe was able to knock over 65-metre frees with ease. He was so accurate and he was already a master of the sideline cut.

'You think the other Cannings are good? Wait until you see the younger brother,' people would say.

Joe was tearing it up in the local leagues. He was just too good for his age. Match after

Joe the Great

match. Minute after minute. Ball after ball. Joe was out of this world. Everything he touched turned to gold. The crowds couldn't believe what they were seeing.

'Who's your man?'

'Look at that lad in the red helmet.'

'I've never seen a young fella like him. He's a natural!'

Joe scored points from the left and right. From in tight and out the field. From the 65s and the sidelines. Not to mention the goals he could score! Nobody had ever seen anything like it before. By the time he was 15, Joe was all set to step up. He was ready for the big time.

Chapter 7

Life Away from the Pitch

Joe was starting to grow and fill out into a fine strong lad. He was always hungry and ate all around him. Sometimes it was a bit of a battle with his mam to make sure he ate all the right healthy foods. She tried to get him to eat plenty of salad and vegetables. He usually cleaned his plate. He knew it was important if he wanted to perform at his best on the pitch.

Joe the Great

Joe was training harder than ever. He was on so many teams in school and his club. He nearly always had a match but he still found room for extra training. A few push-ups here and a few pull-ups there. Every one he could squeeze in would make him stronger and fitter. That would help him get better at hurling.

Joe settled in well at secondary school. It helped that he was so good at hurling. Everyone wanted him on their team. It wasn't just hurling. Joe was always picked first, no matter what game they played in the schoolyard. He was sports mad. He played golf and tennis and even started to play rugby too. He loved the rough and tumble of the game. It was different from hurling and he loved the change.

Another one of Joe's neighbours was John Muldoon, the great Connacht rugby player who was six years older than Joe. John was a hurler before he became a rugby player and had won an All-Ireland minor medal with Galway. John chose to concentrate on rugby when he got

Life Away from the Pitch

older. He would later be Connacht's captain for years. He even got to play for Ireland. John always made time for a puck-about when he came back to Portumna. Joe really looked up to him. He was lucky to have had so many great sportspeople living nearby when he was growing up.

Joe decided to join the local rugby team in Portumna. He loved getting stuck in on the rugby field, especially when it was wet and they would all end up covered in mud from head to toe. Just like in hurling, Joe was magic on the ball. His coaches could see how talented he was. They made him the team's playmaker at number 10. He was big and strong, which was needed for out-half, and loved a tackle. He was the kicker too, as good with his left foot as his right. He was as accurate with an oval ball as he was with a hurley and sliotar. He loved the pressure on his shoulders as he stood over an important kick. It was just the same as taking a free or a 65 in hurling. He would go through the same steps in his mind.

Joe the Great

Take a few deep breaths. Place the ball. Look at the posts. Check the wind. Look at the ball again. Take a few steps back. Take another breath. Start your run-up. Strike the ball.

It almost always ended up over the bar and between the posts. No matter what sport he played, Joe was the man to beat on the pitch.

With so much going on between school, hurling and rugby, Joe had to make sure he didn't get too tired. He had plenty of energy but sometimes he would just crash in the evenings. He wasn't much into video games. During his free time, he would just lie on the sofa and watch some TV or read a book. When he started reading, his eyes would feel tired and he would fall asleep straight away. He loved a good snooze!

Although Joe was hurling crazy, he had plenty of friends away from the pitch. Many of them weren't into sport at all. He liked hanging out and having the craic with them. His friends didn't care about his latest win or score. They treated Joe just like any other lad from Portumna.

Life Away from the Pitch

They would meet up after school and spend some time in the town. They would sit on walls and watch the world go by, or get a few chips, even though Joe knew they weren't very good for him. Sometimes in the summer, they would all go down to the River Shannon and have a swim and splash around.

Joe loved that his friends didn't treat him like a star. It was the perfect way to relax and get away from the pressure of playing well. From an early age, Joe knew that even though sport was special, it wasn't the most important thing in life. Family always came first for Joe, then friends and then hurling. It was only a game at the end of the day.

Chapter 8

The Joe Show

On the pitch, Joe was getting better by the day. He was the main man for his secondary school, Portumna Community School, and usually the biggest player on the pitch. He had the skills to match. Nobody could stop him.

They blitzed their way through the Connacht colleges' hurling season. But they faced a tough match in the final. They were up against St Raphael's from Loughrea, their neighbours and biggest rivals. St Raphael's

The Joe Show

were a great team. They hadn't won the title for six years and wanted it badly.

There wasn't much craic on the bus to Ballinasloe for the final. All the lads had serious faces as they thought about the game ahead.

The pitch at Duggan Park looked fantastic. There was a big crowd there to watch. In the warm-up, Joe picked up a few blades of grass and threw them to the wind. It was blowing strong. The team gathered into a huddle before the game started.

'Ground hurling today, lads. Keep it low and fast,' said their manager.

'We've come a long way this year,' added Joe. 'Don't let it slip now. Fight for everything. Go hard but fair. Chase every ball. When you get a chance, bury it. Come on, lads!' he roared.

His teammates were pumped. The referee threw in the ball. The game was on.

St Raphael's made a flying start and were six points up after just nine minutes. Portumna finally got going but Joe wasted a few easy chances. He was so annoyed with himself.

Joe the Great

'Come on, Joe. You're better than that,' roared his forward partner Steve Duane. 'Chin up!'

The lads from Loughrea were pulling away now. They did some serious damage before half-time. First, Francis Kerrigan found the back of the net after a great solo run. Then full-forward Kevin Hynes scored a second after his shot was dropped by Portumna's goalkeeper.

Portumna were in big trouble.

'It's alright, lads,' said Joe calmly at half-time. 'Only for the goals we're on top. Keep going.'

Joe started the second half at full pelt. He caught every ball, won every tackle and started to find his scoring range. He latched on to a high ball, swung and made a perfect connection. It whistled into the back of the net. The St Raphael's goalkeeper didn't even see it.

'Come on!' shouted Joe, pumping his fist.

They were back in the match.

Soon he had scored another. This time, he ran through the defence, barging players out of

The Joe Show

the way before finding time and space to pick his spot for goal number two. The match was right in the balance now.

St Raphael's came on the attack again. Despite their best efforts, Portumna lost the day. The slow start did the damage as the final score was 3-12 to 2-11. Joe had scored 2-3 but he was angry that he had missed so many chances. It was hard to watch as the Loughrea lads lifted the cup.

***

Despite the disappointment, Joe was soon celebrating again. His fine performances for his school and club meant his talent couldn't be held back any more. One day, when he got home from school, his dad had some news for him.

'There was someone looking for you earlier,' he said.

'Who?' replied Joe.

'A fella called Mattie Murphy. Do you know who he is?'

Joe the Great

'The Galway minor manager? What did he want me for?' asked Joe. He hoped he already knew the answer.

'Well, what do you think?' said his dad with a smile. 'He wants you to play for the minors this year!'

Joe felt a shiver run down his spine. Then he jumped into the air with delight.

Yes! His dream had come true.

'Well done, son!' said his dad with a tear in his eye. 'If you're good enough, you're old enough.'

Joe was still just 15 but everyone in Galway had known about him for some time. Now it was time for the rest of the country to see the Joe Show.

***

Joe burst onto the scene that summer.

Galway swatted aside all their opposition and beat Cork in the semi-final to race into the All-Ireland final. They were up against Kilkenny.

The Joe Show

It was the first of many times Joe would face the mighty Cats.

Joe was a month short of his 16th birthday when he lined out against Kilkenny in the 2004 minor final. It was his first time out on the famous Croke Park pitch and he was so excited. He had dreamed of this day for years, ever since he had played in the field beside his home in Gortanumera. Now he was here, for real.

He took it all in. The smell of the grass. The sounds of the thousands of fans. The sight of Hill 16 and the Cusack stand. It was everything he ever wanted and more.

The match was a tough, tight contest between two evenly matched teams. The Cats were hoping to make it their third win in a row. Galway were determined to stop them. Galway were ahead right to the end, but a last-minute point by 16-year-old Richie Hogan snatched a draw for Kilkenny. The teams would have to meet again in a replay.

Joe didn't have the best of games. He was

Joe the Great

relieved he would get another chance to show just what he could do.

A week later, the two teams came together again in Tullamore. This time the match was even better. Almost 10,000 fans were packed into O'Connor Park, an unbelievable crowd for a minor game. Joe was ready for the action right from the off. He had a feeling it would be their day.

'You threw it away the last day,' roared their manager Mattie Murphy on the pitch before the game. 'Don't let it happen again.'

Kilkenny were playing into a stiff wind but were the better side in the first half. Richie Hogan was their main man again and Galway couldn't get to grips with him. But in the second half it was all about Joe.

Joe cracked four fine points, one after another. One from play, a free and then two skilful sideline cuts. It was the very move he had practised at home for years. Now he had done it on the national stage with everyone watching.

An incredible sideline cut!

The Joe Show

'He's only 15!' gasped one man in the crowd.

'Cracking score, Joe. Keep it going. Keep chasing,' roared his teammate Kerril Wade.

The Cats weren't beaten yet, though. They came roaring back right to the end. Galway didn't score for the last eight minutes. Joe couldn't breathe. The tension was too much. There was just a point in it now but he kept believing, kept running and kept tackling.

Just when they thought they could give no more, the referee finally lifted the whistle to his lips. It was all over.

Galway are the All-Ireland minor champions!

Joe dropped to his knees and looked to the sky. They had done it! In his first year on the team, Galway had won the All-Ireland.

Kerril Wade, Kevin Hynes and Finian Coone all jumped on top of Joe and screamed for joy.

It was one of the finest minor hurling matches of all time. A classic – and Joe had played his part.

Joe the Great

The Galway fans spilled onto the pitch and swarmed around Joe, lifting him into the air. Galway hurling had a new hero. Joe was just getting started.

Chapter 9

Band of Brothers

The club is where it all begins for every player. Every GAA club in the country, big or small, is a community of friends, family and neighbours. They come together to play for the pride of their parish. But Portumna was extra special. It was a band of brothers in more ways than one.

For more than a century, Portumna GAA had nothing much to celebrate. Then the Cannings came along. With Ivan, Ollie, Davy and Frank on the team, they were always hard to beat.

Joe the Great

Now that Joe was coming through to join them, Portumna was growing even stronger.

But it wasn't just the Cannings. For some strange reason, four bands of brothers emerged in the community at the same time. The Lynch, Smith and Hayes families, as well as the Cannings, were all about to play their part in the greatest sporting success the club had ever seen.

Portumna were as close as a team could be. There were reminders everywhere that this was a hurling town. The butcher Eugene McEntee was a leader at the back. Eoin Lynch in the hardware store was a midfield monster. If you wanted to buy a car in the town, it was likely that star players Damien and Niall Hayes would sell it to you. All the talk was hurling, no matter where you went.

They did things like a family too. Before any big match, all the players would gather in the town to hang out with their family and friends and chat about the game. They would have a puck-about on the green beside the church. It

Band of Brothers

was a great way to relax and ease the nerves on a big day.

It hadn't always been this way. The club had some hard times over the years, especially way back in the 1960s. Joe's uncle Frankie was on the team then. There were six Portumna players on the Galway team that year and the future looked bright. But Ireland was a different country at that time. It was very poor and there wasn't much work in east Galway. All six players left the country and emigrated to London to find work. It meant the club lost half a team overnight and it took years to recover. Joe's dad Seán even left to play for nearby Killimor for some time. But his heart was always in Portumna.

When Joe's dad came back, it was time to write a new chapter. Portumna won the intermediate title in 1992 and never looked back.

Off the field, everything changed. Seán retired from playing and became the chairman of the club. Séamus was the treasurer and Uncle Frankie became the selector. They built

Joe the Great

up the club the right way. Now with the Canning, Hayes, Lynch and Smith lads on the pitch, it was time for a new age of glory.

The club's big breakthrough came in 2003, when they won their first ever senior Galway title. They beat their big rivals Loughrea by 2-13 to 2-9. It was a huge moment for Portumna.

Ivan, Ollie, Frank and Davy were all on the team. Joe was still too young to play but he watched on as the heroes arrived home to crazy celebrations. There were bonfires all along the road. His mam Josephine was there with a huge smile on her face. Joe knew that next year he would be part of it all. That night, he promised to himself that he would make the team even better.

The next season was Joe's first on the team. Straight away, he lived up to all expectations. He was in awesome form and helped Portumna get an exciting win over Turloughmore in the Galway semi-final. They were to play against Athenry in the final.

Band of Brothers

Athenry were a strong team with the Cloonan brothers and former county stars Brian Feeney and Joe Rabbitte. In the end, it wasn't to be Joe's day. Athenry were too strong and stopped Portumna winning two in a row. Joe was so disappointed. His first season in the senior team had ended in defeat.

***

The next year was different. Joe was stronger and had become an important player for Portumna, even though he was still just 17. They marched to the final again and came up against old rivals Loughrea once more. More than 13,000 fans poured into Pearse Stadium in Galway to watch the thrilling match. Joe and Damien Hayes were unstoppable on the day.

Joe scored 1-11 and Hayes got 2-6.

Portumna have done it! Galway champions for the second time ever!

The terrible twins Hayes and Canning win the day!

Joe the Great

Joe was in dreamland. But there was more to come.

He fired a fabulous 1-9 in the Connacht final, where they flew past Roscommon champions Four Roads. He scored 1-7 against the Kilkenny club James Stephens in the All-Ireland semi-final. This set up their first ever shot at All-Ireland glory in the final at Croke Park on St Patrick's Day. It was more than anyone could dream of for this small club by the banks of the River Shannon. Yet here they were.

Cork club Newtownshandrum were their opponents on the day. They were also a small club built on strong families. The famous Cork stars Ben and Jerry O'Connor were on the team. It was going to be a tough match.

The team kept up their usual tradition of meeting at the church grounds in Portumna and having a puck-about before they got the bus to Dublin. The whole town turned out to wish them well. Everywhere was covered in blue and yellow flags and banners. None of the players had ever seen excitement like it.

It was a cold, windy day at Croke Park. Joe was getting used to playing at the stadium now but today was extra special. He was here with his brothers, his friends and all his family.

There were no nerves in the dressing room before the match. Joe felt that it was going to be their day. As he pulled on the number 14 Portumna jersey, he thought back to when he was a little boy, dreaming of this moment.

The referee knocked on the dressing-room door. It was time.

'Think of those fans. The support we have is unreal,' said Ollie as they came in for a huddle. 'We can't let them down.'

The players all put their hands together. 'We're brothers. We're a family. We're not losing today,' Ollie finished.

It was a great speech. All the Portumna players felt like they could run through a brick wall.

Joe stood tall in the centre of the pitch. He stood out because of his dyed blond hair. He took one last look around, then clipped on his red helmet. The whistle blew. The game was on.

Just 2 minutes and 20 seconds in, Joe had already made his mark. He sneaked around the back of the Newtownshandrum defence. The ball was slipped inside to him. He held off two strong challenges, using every ounce of muscle on his tall frame. He was in on goal now and his eyes lit up. He drilled a solid shot right down the middle.

Gooooooooaaaaaaallllllll!

The Boy Wonder strikes on the biggest stage of all!

'What a goal, Joe!' said Damien Hayes. 'Now let's have another one!'

Joe then turned provider. He caused all sorts of trouble at the back and dragged the ball across goal to be finished by Niall Hayes.

'Yeesss!' roared Joe.

Nine minutes in and they were two goals up. 'Anything you can do, I can do better!' joked Damien.

'Come on, lads, focus,' roared Davy from out the field. There was still a long way to go.

The Cork side struck back. Jerry O'Connor finished the move of the match at 21 minutes. At half-time, Portumna were ahead but there was still work to do.

Incredibly, Portumna didn't score another point from play in the second half. All their scores came from frees. Who else struck them but Joe Canning? He was as accurate as ever.

Joe worked his socks off. He chased every ball and tackled like his life depended on it.

When he could give no more, the referee blew the final whistle. It was music to Joe's ears.

Portumna are the All-Ireland club champions for the first time in history!

The Tommy Moore Cup is coming back over the Shannon!

Ollie had been brilliant at the back, reading the game, covering and even clearing off the line in the closing stages. Joe had been even better. He was named man of the match and was overcome with joy and relief. He was trying to take it all in. Some people waited their whole lives for a moment like this. Joe hadn't even sat his Leaving Cert yet! He shook his head in disbelief.

In the wild celebrations on the pitch afterwards, Ollie found Joe and the two of them hugged.

'What a feeling!' Ollie whispered into Joe's ear. 'Take it from me, it doesn't get any better than this.'

Goalkeeper Ivan joined them and then half-forward Davy, followed by coach Frank. Their mam and dad, Josephine and Seán, were there too, with their other brother Séamus and sister Deirdre. The Canning brothers stood on the pitch, side by side, celebrating All-Ireland glory with their family, their home, their parish and their town. A band of brothers.

Chapter 10
Setback

Joe was a rising star now. He had the world at his feet and he was enjoying his new-found fame. He signed a boots deal, which meant he didn't have to spend his nights scrubbing the muck from his studs. From now on, he had the pick of the finest boots around. All for free!

He even had his name stitched into the black leather in brilliant white lettering. CANNING.

The following summer, Joe was called up to the Galway senior squad for the first time.

Joe the Great

'Listen, Joe, I would love to have you in the team,' said manager Conor Hayes on the phone. 'I think you're ready.'

'I don't know, Conor. I'm not sure. I have a lot on my plate with the minors, the under-21s and the club,' replied Joe.

'Sure, have a think about it. We'd love to have you,' said Conor as he ended the call.

Joe didn't know what to think. It was a huge honour to be called up. But he wasn't sure he was ready. He asked his whole family for advice. He spoke to the minor manager, Mattie Murphy, too. Joe was the captain of the minor team and he felt he owed it to his teammates to stay on.

In the end, Joe felt the time just wasn't right. He was still too young. With a heavy heart, he turned down the offer. Instead, he decided to stay on with the minors for one more year in the hope of making history and winning three in a row.

***

Setback

Joe's next step up that summer was with the Galway under-21s. It was an All-Ireland semi-final against Kilkenny in Tullamore on a cloudy Saturday night. Joe started on the bench but it wasn't long before he took to the field.

Kilkenny were playing well. They had a great crop of young players like James 'Cha' Fitzpatrick and Richie Power. They were starting to fly out of sight.

Joe barged onto the field and scored a cracking goal with his very first touch. A perfect one-handed finish from a long free in. Then he slotted a couple of beauties from out the field, before scoring a point from his trademark sideline cut. His masterclass continued into the second half as he danced across the grass. It looked like he was playing a different game from everyone else on the pitch.

Kilkenny were panicking and put a new man on to mark him. It made little difference. Joe rasped another into the Kilkenny net.

Goooooooaaaaaaallllllll!

Joe the Great

Have you ever seen anything like it? This kid has it all!

For all his work, Joe wasn't able to change the outcome of the game. Kilkenny still won. Yet all the talk that night was of his performance. He had scored 2-4 in just 40 minutes on the pitch. Now everybody knew all about Joe Canning. He wasn't one for the future anymore. He was a star right now.

***

Two weeks later, Joe was back in Croke Park for the minor final. This time they were facing Tipperary, who were looking for their first title in 10 years. All eyes were on Joe but Galway just never got going on the day. Tipperary had a strong team. They had players like Pádraic Maher and Séamus Callanan coming through.

Joe did what he could to lift his team but they were well beaten on the day. It was his last ever game with the minors and he was gutted it had ended in defeat. Still, he was

Setback

glad he stuck with his teammates and gave it a crack.

***

Joe took a short break after the final. He was able to reflect on the crazy season that had just passed. It had its ups and downs and finished with disappointment. But the club title win on St Patrick's Day was a memory he would have for the rest of his life. Incredibly, he was still just 17. He was on top of the world and felt invincible.

But it all came crashing down in an instant.

Joe was soon back in action for Portumna in a tense club match against their fierce local rivals Loughrea. There was a strange atmosphere at the game. Joe and Ollie had a bad feeling before it even started.

Joe was used to getting some rough treatment on the pitch but this was different. Just a few minutes in, he was knocked to the ground by a heavy front tackle. Suddenly, he got a boot right to his head. The studs stamped right through his face guard, bursting his lip and hurting his eye.

Owwwwwww!

Joe rolled around in agony. There was blood everywhere. A huge row broke out between the players as the doctor ran onto the pitch to treat Joe. Like a true warrior, he managed to play on. He had to get eight stitches at half-time.

He could hardly see. The Portumna players and fans were so angry. Nobody even got a yellow card for the incident. They felt Joe had been singled out on purpose.

The game went on and Loughrea claimed a famous win. But at the final whistle the trouble continued. Five gardaí had to run onto the pitch to escort the referee off. Joe, the Cannings and Portumna were disgusted.

Joe was in so much pain afterwards. His mam was heartbroken to see her little boy's face covered in stitches and glued up. He would have scars for life.

Setback

'How are you feeling now, love?' his mam asked him.

Joe wasn't in the mood for talking. His lip was so painful when he tried to speak.

'I'm okay, Mam. Don't worry about me,' he managed to say.

The incident really upset Joe. He felt like quitting hurling for good. His father had always told him, 'Play hard and play fair.' This wasn't how the game was supposed to be played. Joe didn't want to go on if this kind of thing could happen. He decided to take a few weeks off to recover. He thought long and hard about whether he would play on. Everyone in Galway was worried that their star player was about to walk away from the game he loved.

Chapter 11

Bouncing Back

Joe moved to Limerick when he finished secondary school. He started a course in business and marketing in college in Limerick, and he was happy to be away from the limelight. The wound on his face had healed but he was still upset about the rough treatment he had received in the Galway county final. He wanted to rest for a while and let it go away. So, he decided to once again turn down a call-up to the Galway senior team.

Bouncing Back

He was angry that the county board hadn't done more to protect him or punish the player who hurt him. This was Joe's way of standing up for himself. It was a huge blow to Galway.

While in Limerick, Joe started to play some rugby again. He even got an offer to play for the local team, Shannon RFC, one of the biggest clubs in Ireland. They had heard he was taking a break from hurling and wanted him to join them. Joe was tempted but decided to turn down the offer in the end. He just wanted to be a normal teenager for a while and enjoy life.

***

It wasn't long before his love of hurling pulled him back to the sport again. Joe was living in a house with a great group of GAA players. Limerick's Paudie O'Brien and David Slattery from Kildare were there, along with Nicky Cleere from Kilkenny and Tipperary's Shane McGrath. They had some craic hanging around or going for a game of golf. They were sports mad and were always challenging each other to competitions and games. They would watch matches together, whether it was soccer, rugby or football. Most of the time, the talk was about hurling. It gave Joe the itch to get started again.

Joe eventually returned to the LIT team for the Fitzgibbon Cup. They were led by legendary manager Davy Fitzgerald. Davy ran a tight ship and training was tough. The lads woke up at six in the morning to go training before college. With Joe back on the side, they were a match for anyone.

LIT played their way into the final against NUI Galway. It was strange for Joe to be playing against a team from Galway. He knew plenty of the lads he was up against but he never lost his focus. Today was all about winning a second Fitzgibbon Cup for LIT.

They got just the start they wanted. Aonghus Callanan, who also played with Joe on the Galway team, smashed the ball into the back of the net.

Bouncing Back

'Yeess, Aonghus!' roared Joe. 'What a finish! Come on, lads!'

LIT were much the better team and, in a dramatic spell, won a penalty just before half-time.

Joe stepped up, took aim and fired.

What a save by David Woods!

'How did he keep it out?' Joe looked to the heavens. He couldn't believe it.

But right at the start of the second half, Joe got it right. This time, Callanan did the hard work. He set Joe up for a simple finish.

Gooooooooaaaaaaalllllll!

Joe pumped his fists and leaped into the air. Aonghus jumped on his back. They knew they had won it now.

'Do I have to do everything?' laughed Aonghus. 'I laid that one on a plate for you. It couldn't have been easier.'

'Haha! You would've missed it,' replied Joe cheekily.

It was a great feeling. Joe was the top scorer again with 1-8 and they eventually won

Joe the Great

by 2-16 to 0-13. They celebrated on the pitch long after the final whistle.

Joe was so happy as they lifted the cup. He had tasted success before but this somehow seemed more enjoyable. It was great to just be out there playing with his friends.

As Joe stood for a photo with goalkeeper James Skehill and forward Iarla Tannian, Davy Fitzgerald approached him. He grabbed him into a strong hug and whispered in his ear.

'You have the stuff, Joe. You've all the right stuff. You're one of the finest hurlers in the game. I hope Galway look after you. Because if they do, I know you'll look after them.'

With Davy's words ringing in his ear, Joe made a strong return to the Galway under-21s that summer. They blitzed Dublin in the All-Ireland final at Croke Park by a remarkable 5-11 to 0-12. Joe chipped in with 3 points in front of a crowd of 33,000. He was getting used to this winning feeling. It was a further sign that Galway had a great crop of young players that could go on to have success in the years ahead.

Bouncing Back

Joe's underage days were over now. It was finally time for him to shine at the highest level and to take his rightful place at the heart of the Galway senior team. It was a moment he had been waiting for since the day he was born.

Chapter 12
All Star

Joe was now 19 years old. He was already a famous hurler. Many people thought he was one of the stars of the game. Yet he still hadn't played a senior game for Galway. That was about to change.

It was a national league semi-final against Cork at the Gaelic Grounds in Limerick. It was a familiar pitch for Joe. Galway manager Ger Loughnane named him at corner-forward. Joe was so excited. He was nervous too but he

All Star

knew he was ready for the step up this time.

He looked around the dressing room. There were plenty of familiar faces. Joe had played with most of the lads before, at under-21 level or college. Hayes, Skehill and Hynes were all there.

'Let's go, Joe,' said Skehill as they walked through the tunnel. 'This is it now. Show them what you can do.'

Joe took a deep breath and stepped onto the pitch.

He made a nervous start for the first 15 minutes and felt a little panicked. Everything was faster, more intense. This was different. He was up against the best players from other counties now and this Cork team was very strong.

'Relax, Joe!' roared Hayes. 'Don't force it.'

Eventually he got on the end of a ball in, slipping his marker and slotting over a fine point.

A first point for the Boy Wonder! He's up and running at senior level!

Joe the Great

Joe felt the weight lift from his shoulders. He started to do his thing. A clever hand pass found Iarla Tannian, who smashed home the opening goal.

'Great ball, Joe. That's the stuff,' shouted Tannian.

Joe then added another point before half-time with a quick-fire pull that sent the ball over the bar. Cork's goalkeeper Donal Óg Cusack was relieved to see it flash over.

He scored another couple of points in the second half, one twisting off his left-hand side and then a great sideline cut.

Whoooosh!

He lofted the ball 50 yards and high over the bar. It was Joe's speciality. He had done it so many times before but now the whole country was watching.

The Galway fans cheered. Their new hero had arrived. Galway won the game by 2-22 to 0-24. They were off to the league final.

'Congrats, Joe. You're up and running now!' Loughnane congratulated him afterwards.

All Star

'It's a lot different to club games. The speed of it,' said Joe, puffing out his cheeks. 'But it's good to get the first one out of the way.'

In his heart he was really proud, but he wasn't showing it. Afterwards, his mam and dad had a big hug for him. Their little boy was all grown up.

Galway lost the final by two points to Tipperary, who were much better on the day. But Joe was singled out for praise again. Just two games in and he was already becoming the main man. Little did anyone know he was about to get even better.

***

One of the greatest performances ever seen on a hurling pitch came from Joe on 19 July 2008. It's a date that will always be remembered in GAA history. Cork were Galway's opponents once again. This time, it was in the championship. Nobody in Semple Stadium in Thurles that evening would ever forget what they saw. It was a game for the ages.

Joe the Great

The sun was shining. The fans were in full voice before the start. Joe felt it was going to be a special game. He pulled on his famous red helmet and looked to the sky. It was showtime.

It took just 10 minutes for Joe to begin his show. He reached high to pluck the sliotar out of the sky and used all his strength to wriggle away from Diarmuid 'The Rock' O'Sullivan.

O'Sullivan was one of the best defenders in the game.

Joe still had a lot of work to do. He faced the amazing talents of Cork goalkeeper Donal Óg. Joe was under huge pressure but he managed to free his hand and slap a genius one-handed shot. It took everyone by surprise.

Gooooooooaaaaaaalllllll!

Joe Canning! Back of the net! A wonderful goal!

Joe didn't stop there. He pointed another couple of frees and then won a dramatic penalty. Donal Óg was sent off for the incident.

The crowd came to a standstill. Joe stepped up to take the penalty.

All Star

Gooooooooaaaaaaalllllll!
What a penalty by Canning! He wasn't going to miss that!

Cork were in big trouble by half-time. It seemed that Galway only had one player on the pitch. Joe had scored all of Galway's two goals and five points.

Joe was fouled every time he went for the ball. He continued to knock over the frees. He was causing havoc. Cork put on a new man to mark him but it made no difference. Joe bounced out of a tackle between John Gardiner and Seán Óg Ó'hAilpín and fired a fierce shot off his left-hand side.

Strong, powerful and deadly accurate!

Then he threw in a sideline cut, his trademark.

Look at it! Like a plane taking off and landing again. He can do no wrong!

The only problem for Joe was that Cork kept scoring at the other end too. Every time Joe knocked over another one, Cork came back. It looked like Joe would have to do it on his own. The one-man attack.

Joe the Great

With 10 minutes to play, Galway trailed by a goal. Joe closed the gap again with another daring point from out the field.

A real Cú Chulainn of a man! Has anyone ever seen a performance like this?!

Joe raised his hands in the air to pump up the crowd. They roared back with excitement.

Both teams went at it again in the final stages. Galway were running out of steam. Eventually the final whistle blew. Cork had won it.

It was one of the most exciting games ever but Joe fell to his knees. He couldn't believe he had lost.

Joe couldn't have done any more. He finished the game having scored 2 goals and 12 points out of Galway's total score of 2-15. It was something that had never been seen before.

His brother Ollie was playing at full-back that day. He walked up to Joe but had nothing to say. There were no words. He just gave his

All Star

little brother a hug. Even though Galway had lost, everyone knew they had seen a genius at work that day. At the age of 19, the Portumna Prodigy was well on his way to greatness.

Joe finished the season with an All Star and was named Young Player of the Year. It was just the reward he deserved.

Chapter 13
The King v the Prince

Although Joe was making big waves, he still wasn't the best hurler in the country. That honour went to Kilkenny's king, Henry Shefflin. For now, Joe was just the prince.

King Henry had won everything that could be won in the game. He was the star of the unstoppable Kilkenny team. Many said they were the best team to ever play. By the time Shefflin retired, he had won 10 All-Irelands, 13 Leinster titles, 6 national leagues and 11 All Stars. He was a true great.

The King v the Prince

Joe had always looked up to Henry. Now he had a chance to rub shoulders with him on the pitch, to go head-to-head with the greatest player of his generation. Portumna reached the All-Ireland club semi-finals again. There they would meet Shefflin's club, Ballyhale Shamrocks, from Kilkenny. It was a huge test for Joe. Everybody was talking about the clash between the king and the prince.

'Don't mind all that. It's only nonsense,' Joe's brother Ivan told him in the build-up to the big game. But it was playing on Joe's mind. It was his chance to show everybody he was just as good as Henry.

The Portumna band of brothers gathered again on the green, as they always did before setting off for Semple Stadium. Kevin 'Chunky' Hayes was messing about with his cousins Damien and Niall. Brothers Leo and Andy Smith were pucking a ball against the church wall.

Of course, the Cannings were back together again. Ivan, Ollie and Joe made up the spine of the team. It was some line-up. But Ballyhale

Shamrocks were a serious team too, with plenty of threats other than Shefflin.

'Lads, it's all about the fast start. We've been working on it all week,' explained manager Johnny Kelly in the huddle just before throw-in. 'Keep an eye on Henry at all times. He's the danger man. Make sure you get out of the traps early,' he said, shaking his fist.

That's exactly what Portumna did. Straight away, the terrible twins Damien Hayes and Joe Canning made a perfect start by scoring a goal each in the opening minutes. Ballyhale Shamrocks were rocked. Henry stepped up and stuck over some simple frees. It steadied their nerves and got them back in the game. Portumna came again. Joe was at the heart of it as always, showing off his creative skill.

Goooooooaaaaaaalllllll!
Joe Canning! A lovely flicked finish!

Joe finished the half with another perfect sideline cut. His team were 3-7 to 1-7 ahead.

But the great Shefflin wasn't going to let them win so easily. Ballyhale Shamrocks scored

The King v the Prince

six points in a row, five from the king himself. They were right back in it. It was tight and tense.

Towards the end, Portumna went up another gear. Ollie kept things tight at the back. It meant the forwards were free to do the damage. With the game in the balance, Joe burst through and crashed a thunderbolt against the crossbar. The sliotar flashed back out to Ciaran Ryan, who struck home the rebound.

Gooooooooaaaaaaalllllll!

'Yes, Ryan!' shouted Joe.

'You did the hard work, Joe!' he laughed back.

The goals won the game for Portumna.

They jumped for joy at the final whistle. The Canning, Hayes and Smith brothers and the rest of the lads were on their way to another All-Ireland final at Croke Park. Their star man Joe had put King Henry Shefflin in the shade.

Joe had finished with the perfect set of scores: a goal from play, a penalty, two points from 65s, a point from a free, a point from play and a point from a sideline cut. A full house. The prince was showing all the signs that one day he would be king.

Portumna went on to win the All-Ireland final against Waterford's De La Salle.

***

When the summer came, it was time for the king and the prince to meet again. Canning would face Shefflin as Galway came up against the mighty Kilkenny Cats in the Leinster semi-final.

Again, all the talk was about Joe and Henry. Who would come out on top? It was Joe's first championship clash against this great Kilkenny team. It was going to be his toughest test yet. He would be marked by one of the greatest defenders of them all, J.J. Delaney. Joe was thinking about it for the whole week before the match. He knew he would be in for a right battle.

The King v the Prince

On the day, it made little difference who marked Joe. Nobody could stop him. He was on fire that day.

Joe proved that his performance the year before against Cork wasn't a one-off. The match was only just warming up when Joe gave J.J. the slip and ran like the wind towards the Kilkenny goal. J.J. chased him but he couldn't catch Joe. Joe fired out a rasping shot.

Gooooooooaaaaaaalllllll!

He bagged another early in the second half. This time it was an unstoppable free from out the field. Most other players would have stuck it over the bar, but not Joe. He only had eyes for the goal.

What a young player he is! So talented!

But just like the year before, Joe couldn't do it all on his own. Henry was in flying form and fired over 10 points. Joe might have been the best player on the pitch but Kilkenny were the better team. Thanks to manager Brian Cody, they just didn't know how to lose. The Cats fought back to win by four points.

Joe the Great

Joe was heartbroken. He stood in the centre of the pitch on his own wondering how Galway had lost again.

Henry Shefflin saw him and made his way towards him. The Kilkenny fans were jumping around on the pitch and giving Henry high fives. But he walked up to Joe to shake his hand and pat him on the back.

'Fair play, Joe. Great game,' said Henry.

'Thanks, Henry, you were better than us in the end.' Joe was upset but knew it was important to lose with dignity.

'You're some player, Joe,' said Henry. 'Your day will come. Don't worry about that. You'll have plenty to celebrate if you keep playing like that.' Henry leaned across and hugged Joe.

It was a great sight. The two best players in the game standing shoulder to shoulder, sharing a moment after a hard-fought game. The king and the prince.

Chapter 14
Injury

Joe had been on the go for a while now. Even though he was still young, he had been playing at the top level for five years with club, college and county. It suddenly started to catch up with him. He had been struggling with a few small injuries during the season but now they were getting serious. He had a sore heel that made it hard for him to run properly. He also had some pain in his hip and down the side of his leg.

Joe the Great

'You need a rest,' said the physio as Joe lay stretched out on the table. 'Your body can only take so much.'

It wasn't what Joe wanted to hear. 'That's not even an option,' he thought to himself. Galway needed him. His teammates were counting on him.

'Just see what you can do,' he said to the physio.

Over the next few months, Joe visited many doctors to see if they could fix his problems. He found an expert in Cork who said he could help Joe to put his injuries behind him.

'Sure, I've nothing to lose,' said Joe. 'I might as well go for it.'

Joe visited the expert every day for the first week. He would crack Joe's joints and muscles and move them all about.

Owwwwwww!

Joe could feel the pain running through his body but he was hopeful it would do the job.

Joe's injuries stopped him from training and he had a stop-start season. Portumna reached

Injury

the All-Ireland club final again but lost. Henry Shefflin's Ballyhale Shamrocks finally got their revenge. It was a tough defeat for Joe to take.

Joe bounced back for Galway in the national league. He topped the scoring charts as they beat Cork in the final. Joe was the hero of the day with a total haul of 1-5. It was a great moment.

Galway were now one of the hot favourites for the All-Ireland in the summer. But it didn't work out that way.

Joe was struggling for form and fitness in the run-up to the Leinster final. Galway once again came up against the mighty Kilkenny. Joe had a day to forget, scoring just two points. The Cats were worthy winners. King Henry was the class act on the pitch once more, scoring 1-7.

Joe was starting to get sick of the sight of him.

Things only got worse for Galway. They crashed out of the All-Ireland series in a narrow defeat to Tipperary in the quarter-final.

Joe the Great

Joe scored 1-5 but was far from his best. He started to get some criticism from fans.

'Joe hasn't kicked on.'

'He's going backwards.'

'He's burned out.'

It seemed everyone had an opinion on Joe Canning. When Galway won, they thought he was great. But if Galway lost, it seemed to Joe that it was all his fault.

Joe was living in Dublin now with a full-time job. He was finding it hard to drive up and down to training and matches. He felt tired and worn out all the time. He missed his family too.

One night, he drove home to Gortanumera to see his mam and dad.

'I'm struggling, Dad,' he said over a cup of tea at the kitchen table.

'I know, son. Don't worry,' replied his dad kindly. 'You might just need a break.'

'It's not the injuries, though. I'm just not enjoying it anymore,' said Joe. 'Hurling used to mean everything to me. But what's the point if it only makes me feel bad?'

Injury

'Look, if you need to take a rest then take a rest, Joe,' said his mam. 'We all love you and will support you no matter what.'

'Thanks, Mam,' said Joe as he looked up from his mug of tea. 'It's just every time we lose it feels like it's my fault.'

'We're all with you, Joe, no matter what you decide,' said his dad. 'Me, your mam, your sister and all your brothers. We're behind you.'

'Thanks, Dad. I know,' said Joe.

Joe went to sleep that night in his old bed, where he used to dream about playing for Galway. Now he was thinking of packing it all in. No more Joe Show. No more Portumna Prodigy. He thought of living a normal life again, where nobody knew his name or his business.

As Joe's head hit the pillow, something deep down inside him told him he had to go on.

Chapter 15
Master Craftsman

Joe always loved making his own hurleys. Away from the pitch, his favourite place to go was the workshop. He would spend hours there, cutting, carving and sanding, making hurley after hurley. All those years spent watching Tony Keady at work had rubbed off on him. He learned the old skills that had been passed on for years and years. He knew how to pick out the right ash tree and cut it down to size. Bringing it back to the workshop, he knew to measure twice and

Master Craftsman

cut once. He loved the blending and shaping of the wood, working with the natural grain and sanding it to the smoothest finish. He could feel the history in his hands.

When Joe was making his own hurleys, he was very fussy and knew exactly what he wanted. It was all in the feel, weight and balance.

'The three most important things,' Tony would tell him, 'are the weight, the shape and the size.'

Joe always made sure his hurley weighed 600 grams. It needed a good balance, not too heavy on the bottom or at the handle. Not too much spring, either. It was all about how it felt.

Only Joe knew when it was finished and ready for the road. He would fall in love with one and keep it all year just for games. He would never use it in training in case it broke. He would bring 3 to a game and keep 10 at home. He always thought you could never have enough. For Joe, the hurley was like another arm.

Joe the Great

Things were hard in Ireland at the time. Life was difficult for many. There wasn't much money around and jobs were hard to find, especially in east Galway. It was hard for some of Joe's brothers to find work.

'I have an idea,' Joe said to Ivan on the phone one night.

'I'm always worried when you have an idea,' laughed Ivan. 'Go on.'

'Well, I was thinking,' said Joe, 'maybe we could set up our own business, making hurleys.'

'I think that would be mighty!' Ivan jumped in straight away. 'Do you think it would work?'

'I think we can make a go of it. Only one way to find out, sure,' said Joe hopefully.

'Canning Hurleys. I like the sound of that,' joked Ivan.

The two brothers set up their business in a workshop out the back of Ivan's house in Portumna. There was a lot of competition with other hurley makers. They had their work cut out for them. They made each hurley exactly to order.

Master Craftsman

Joe got a few of his Galway teammates on board straight away. Players from other counties started to buy them too. Gavin O'Mahony and Paudie O'Brien from Limerick were some of the players who bought them. Word quickly spread and soon they were very busy.

Joe and Ivan spent days in the workshop together. Joe loved the work. Ivan would mark and cut out the hurleys. Joe's favourite job was sanding and shaping. He would be covered in dust from head to toe.

It was great to be back home with all his family and friends calling to the workshop during the day. He got great satisfaction seeing a product made from start to finish. He loved when a young lad would leave with a new hurley in his hand, just like Joe in Tony Keady's workshop years before. The best thing was he had no boss! He was able to duck out whenever he needed for training.

Spending time back at home, where it all began for Joe, made him think about the future. Now that he was back with his family, his love for hurling slowly came back. He knew he had much more to give. When Joe was winning everything as a minor and under-21, he never thought playing senior would be so hard. He never thought he would go so long without success. All the defeats had taken their toll on him.

It was six years since Galway last made the All-Ireland semi-finals. Joe knew they were still a talented bunch of players. They had so much success together when they were young. It was hard to put their finger on where it was going wrong. He decided it was time to find out. It wasn't going to be easy but Joe was determined to bring Galway back to the top.

Chapter 16
Replay

Joe trained harder than ever over the winter. He went to the gym, ate well, recovered and trained again. He lost a stone in weight and became a yard quicker. His injuries were behind him now. He was fit and ready for a new season. He showed his teammates the right way to prepare off the field, leading by example.

Galway had a new manager too, Anthony Cunningham. They were more determined than ever that this would be their year.

Joe the Great

Galway beat Westmeath and Offaly to set up a Leinster final clash with their old rival Kilkenny. Nobody gave Galway much of a chance. The Cats had been the best team in Ireland for some time now. Galway had been hit and miss for the last few years. But this day was different.

'I'm sick of losing to this lot,' said Joe in the dressing room. He was a leader in the team now and gave an inspiring speech. 'Give it your all. Don't stop. We have the talent. We have the fitness. We can do this!'

They charged onto the field and into the match. Kilkenny didn't know what hit them.

Just three minutes in, Iarla Tannian fired a long ball to the edge of the square. Joe plucked it from the sky, burst past Jackie Tyrell and blasted it home.

What a goal! What a start! Big Joe Canning!

Galway kept their foot on the gas. They scored 1-6 in the first 20 minutes. They kept Kilkenny scoreless until Henry Shefflin got them going with a free. It was a terrible first half for Kilkenny. They trailed by 2-12 to 4 points. Nobody could believe what they were seeing.

Where has this Galway come from?

The Cats showed the spirit of champions and battled back hard. Goals from Richie Hogan and Shefflin put them right back in it. But Joe steadied the ship for Galway again. He slotted two more points.

'Come on, lads. Keep running. Every ball matters now,' he roared to his teammates.

Galway dug in for the closing stages and won by 10 points. Joe was the hero again, scoring 1-10. The mighty Kilkenny had been beaten.

Galway are the 2012 Leinster champions for the very first time! History has been made!

Joe lifted his eyes to the sky and smiled from ear to ear. He stood for a photo in the centre of Croke Park. His longtime friend Iarla Tannian was on one side. Young Niall Donohoe was on the other. Niall was a tough defender from the tiny parish of Kilbeacanty. He was having a stunning first season on the team. He was an All Star in the making.

Joe was in the middle with his arms in the air, his trademark red helmet in one hand and his hurley in the other. The three of them had huge grins on their faces. They were on top of the world.

They had worked hard for this and were going to enjoy it. But already Joe had his eye on a bigger prize.

'Well done, lads. Super game!' the boss congratulated the players as they left the pitch.

In the dressing room, Joe had another message.

'Enjoy it, lads. Days like today don't come around too often. We've beaten the best team now. This year we're going all the way.'

The players cheered and danced in a circle.

It was a special moment.

***

Replay

They continued their flying form in the All-Ireland semi-final against Cork. Joe scored another eleven points, including five frees and two 65s.

When the final whistle blew, the emotion poured out of Joe. He pumped his fist and roared. He was back to his best and Galway were finally into an All-Ireland final. The only problem was they had to play Kilkenny again.

The excitement in Galway was off the charts in the build-up to the big day. Thousands of Galway fans made their way to Croke Park on a beautiful sunny day. Joe took in the sights and sounds on the bus to the stadium. He had been here so many times but never for an All-Ireland final. This was different.

Joe had never heard anything like the roar of the crowd as he walked onto the pitch. The national anthem was played. He felt a shiver go down his spine. He had dreamed of this moment all his life. He was finally here.

The ball was thrown in and the game was on. Joe didn't take long to find his stride.

Just nine minutes in, he caught the sliotar at full pace and charged straight at the Kilkenny backs. He ran right, then turned left, leaving the defenders on the floor. In the blink of an eye, he flashed a fearsome shot right down the middle.

Gooooooooaaaaaaaalllllll!

He's scored a wonderful goal! How did he do that?

Joe's touch and vision were bang on that day. By half-time, he had already scored 1-6 and Galway were 5 points ahead.

Then came the Kilkenny backlash. Henry Shefflin scored point after point after point. But the men from the west came again. A fine goal from Niall Burke made sure it was game on. The Cats fired back.

It was such a tight game. With seconds left, Galway were behind by just one point.

The referee blew his whistle. It was a free in to Galway, far out on the left-hand side.

It was a tough one. Joe stood over it. He needed to score to force a replay. The hopes of the entire county were on his shoulders.

Replay

Over the bar!
Canning saves the day for Galway! It's a replay!

***

Two weeks later, it was back to Croke Park to do it all again. More than 82,000 people packed in to see the drama unfold. Galway's team were unchanged, even though James Skehill got a knock during training. Kilkenny brought in two new players.

They picked up right where they left off in the first match. Joe scored the opening point from a free. A flurry of early goals sparked the game to life. David Burke smashed two for Galway. Then Richie Power blasted home for Kilkenny. At half-time, the Cats were ahead by four points.

Kilkenny were the better side after the break but Galway hung in there. Joe fizzed in a shot that bounced off the post.

'Unlucky, Joe,' roared Burke.

Joe the Great

But two quick goals put an end to Galway's hopes. First Walter Walsh and then Colin Fennelly found the back of the net. Johnny Glynn scored a goal in the 66th minute but it was too little too late. The final whistle blew. Kilkenny were the All-Ireland champions once more.

Joe's stomach sank. He dropped his head and his hurl. Another year gone. Another chance missed. He felt he was never going to win the All-Ireland. He stayed on the pitch and shook hands but he wanted to be anywhere else. It broke his heart to watch Kilkenny lift the Liam MacCarthy Cup once more.

At the end of the season, Joe was named an All Star again. Shefflin beat him to the Player of the Year award. Joe couldn't believe that Shefflin now had nine All-Irelands. He still had none. Would his day ever come?

Chapter 17
Tragedy

The bad news came out of the blue. Nobody expected it. Galway's young wing-back Niall Donohue had died suddenly. He had been nominated for an All Star the year before and had a bright future at the heart of the team. Everyone said he was going to be one of the game's great defenders.

Niall died just before his 23rd birthday. Galway hurling was rocked by the loss. The entire county came together in grief. His local

Joe the Great

GAA club in Kilbeacanty said he was their son, brother, friend and hero. He was the heart of the club.

Joe was so upset when he heard the news. All his teammates were too. They couldn't believe it. Just the year before, they had stood together celebrating the famous day they beat Kilkenny in the Leinster final. Now Niall was gone.

On the day of his funeral, his teammates lined the streets of the village and carried his coffin. They were a family and they had lost a brother.

Niall's death had a terrible effect on Joe and all his teammates. It was hard to focus on hurling when something like this had happened. Joe sometimes wondered if it was worth playing on at all.

But the tragedy brought all the lads closer together. They found it good to train as a group. It helped to clear their heads. They also promised to talk to each other a lot more and share how they were feeling. They helped each other

Tragedy

through the dark days of winter. Soon, they were looking forward to another summer of hurling.

One evening during pre-season, Joe got a phone call.

'How are things, Joe? Do you have a minute to chat?' It was Galway manager Anthony Cunningham.

'Yeah, no bother. What's up?' asked Joe.

'Well, there's no point beating around the bush,' said Anthony. 'I want you to be our captain this year. We'd love to have you lead the team.'

Joe was surprised. He didn't want to commit straight away.

'Wow. Thanks, Anthony. I'm really honoured,' he said, stumbling over his words. 'Can I have a bit of time to think about it?'

'Absolutely, Joe. No bother,' said Anthony. 'Take your time. I think you're a natural leader and we need you.'

Joe hung up the phone. He was worried he had sounded ungrateful. It was a huge honour for him, his family and the club in Portumna.

Joe the Great

He had done it before for the minors and under-21s, but those campaigns had ended in defeat. He was used to leading the team on the pitch, taking games by the scruff of the neck and scoring the winning goals. But he never thought of himself as a natural captain.

He rang his brother Ollie for advice. Ollie had led Galway in the past and he told Joe he'd help him through it. He also rang Frank, who said he could see the reasons for not taking it.

'You've enough on your plate being the team's top scorer,' he said.

Joe thought long and hard about it. He decided to accept the job.

'You don't get asked to captain your county every day,' he said to himself.

Things didn't go well for Galway on the pitch that year. They struggled to a narrow win over Laois in their first Leinster game. Joe only scored two points. It was a sign that something was wrong.

They improved for the next round against Kilkenny. Joe scored 2-3 but it ended in a draw.

Tragedy

They were blown away in the replay. Again, Joe only scored one point, a single sideline cut. Kilkenny won by eight points. Galway's run that year came to a sudden halt early in July with a big loss to Tipperary.

It was a season to forget and another year without silverware for Joe.

'Maybe I'm not meant to be the captain after all,' he thought.

Joe never felt right in the job. Maybe the team just weren't able to give their all after the tragedy of losing one of their key men. Joe's head was spinning as he tried to make sense of the year that had passed. For some reason, he didn't feel as disappointed as he had in other years.

For the first time in a long time, Joe realised there were more important things in life than hurling. He was healthy and happy. He had good family and friends around him. Right now, that was all that mattered.

Chapter 18

Portumna Party

Even though things were going badly on the county scene, Joe enjoyed playing at home with the club. He was able to play without pressure there, with his friends and family. They hadn't had much success recently, so his older brother Frank took over as manager to try to get them back to the top again. With Ollie as captain, Ivan and Joe all playing together, it was a real family affair.

In Frank's first year in charge, they were

Portumna Party

back in the Galway county final. Their bitter rivals Loughrea were their opponents once more. It was the talk of the town in the week running up to the game.

'Stick it to Loughrea on Sunday, Joe.'

'You better be ready for them lads this time.'

'You'll beat them easy, Joe. Not a bother to you!'

Wherever he was, Joe could feel the excitement in the air. More than 9,000 people came to Pearse Stadium on a cold but sunny day in October 2013. It had been four years since Portumna had made it to the final. They were hungrier than ever.

'I played in seven finals in a row,' said Frank as he began his pre-match talk in the dressing room. 'I thought it would go on forever but it finally came to an end. I realise now how special these days are. Don't waste the chance. Win today and you'll be legends in Portumna for the rest of your lives.'

Captain Ollie chipped in too. 'I'm getting older, lads. I won't have many more chances.

Joe the Great

Don't leave anything behind today. Chase every ball. Run your hearts out. And when you get a chance, stick it over the bar.'

Joe was fired up. He was playing for his brothers, his sister, his mam and dad. He was playing for all his family and friends, for Gortanumera and Portumna. He was out for revenge against Loughrea.

Joe set the tone for the day early on. After eight minutes, he stood over a free. Everyone thought he would knock it over the bar. Joe had other ideas. He spotted a gap, took aim and fired.

Goooooooaaaaaaalllllll!

It was a perfect start for Portumna. Loughrea hit back with points from Johnny O'Loughlin, Jamie Ryan and Neil Keary. Just before half-time, Loughrea took another blow. Ollie passed to Damien Hayes, who slipped it to Andy Smith.

Goooooooaaaaaaalllllll!
An excellent goal!

Both teams were level at the break. This

Portumna Party

tough battle could go either way. Joe took charge early in the second half, hurling from out the field and sticking over two vital points. Smith and Ollie added another point each. Then the Hayes brothers got in on the act. Niall set up Damien, who blasted home.

Gooooooooaaaaaaalllllll!

Portumna were the Galway champions once more! Ollie climbed the steps to lift the Tom Callanan Cup. The Portumna players celebrated like their first win back in 2003.

Ollie grabbed Joe with a tight squeeze. 'We're going to enjoy this one!'

'We haven't had a day like this for years,' laughed Joe.

***

Portumna marched on to the All-Ireland club final once more and faced Mount Leinster Rangers from Carlow on St Patrick's Day 2014. It was the Carlow team's first ever All-Ireland final. Portumna were the hot favourites.

Joe the Great

Frank gave another inspirational speech before the game.

'They're a good team. They're dangerous if you give them space. We're better, though. You have the experience, lads. You have the hurling. Go out and show them what you can do and you'll be All-Ireland champions by the end of the game.'

The Portumna players roared. They were up for this one.

Mount Leinster made the better start and grabbed some early points. But once Portumna hit their stride there was only ever going to be one winner. Joe was deadly with frees and Ollie hit three points himself. They were ahead by nine points to five at the break.

It was more of the same afterwards. Joe had a rasping shot from 20 metres blocked on the line but the Hayes brothers added five points between them. Long before the game's end, Portumna knew it would be their day.

The referee blew his whistle.

Portumna Party

Portumna are the All-Ireland club champions! Once again the Cannings are at the heart of it!

Frank, Ollie, Ivan and Joe stood for the cameras holding four fingers in the air. They were All-Ireland club champions for the fourth time.

The lads danced and sang in the dressing room. They had mighty craic on the bus home. Bonfires were lit as they crossed the River Shannon. It was one of the best moments of Joe's life. There was nothing quite like a Portumna party!

Joe took a moment for himself, away from the singing and dancing. He had achieved more than most players could ever dream of. But still he thought about the one trophy he had yet to win. Would he swap it all for just one taste of All-Ireland glory with Galway?

Chapter 19

The Cats Again

Joe hadn't enjoyed being captain the year before. When the Galway squad got together for another season, there was no mention of who would lead the side. Joe soon found out that David Collins was the new captain. He was a bit annoyed he hadn't been told but he was free now to get back to doing what he did best. Scoring.

Galway tore into the new championship season. They fought out a draw with Dublin

The Cats Again

on their first day out, but made no mistake in the replay. Joe scored two goals in a thumping win 5-19 to 1-18. They hammered Laois in their next game with a final score of 3-28 to 1-14. Joe scored a crazy 1-15. He was up and running now.

Galway were into the Leinster final once more. Of course, their rivals on the day would be Kilkenny yet again. Many people said the Cats were on the slide. They said they weren't the great team they had once been. Joe's great rival over the years, King Henry Shefflin, had called it a day and retired in March 2015.

No team could survive the loss of one of the greatest players of all time. But they were still a strong side and were led by one of the best managers in the game, Brian Cody. Cody was chasing his 38th title in a remarkable career.

Galway defended like lions early on. After 27 minutes, the Cats finally found the back of the net thanks to T.J. Reid. The Tribesmen were up against it and needed something special.

Joe the Great

Luckily, they had just the player to turn to.

Joe put his hand in the air. He signalled to Andy Smith that he wanted it in high. Smith fired a long pass from deep inside his own half, to where Joe was waiting on the edge of the square. It was perfectly placed, right behind the Kilkenny defence.

What happened next stunned everyone on the pitch and everyone watching at home on TV. Joe had his back to goal but caught the ball in his left hand. He spun like a ballerina to face goal. He swung his stick with his right hand in one swift move. The big man moved with such grace. He was light on his feet and fast as a flash. Whoosh! Joe cracked the sliotar right past goalkeeper Eoin Murphy.

Brilliant catch! Oh my God! What a gooooooooaaaaaaalllllll!

Joe Canning! How does he do it?

Joe slapped his hurley with his hand and pumped his fist. He was roaring at his teammates through the face guard on his famous red helmet. It was one of the greatest

The Cats Again

goals the game of hurling had ever seen. Another one for the Joe Canning collection.

But the same story of Joe's career would continue that day. Despite his best efforts, Kilkenny won in the end. There was just no beating this team.

***

Galway regrouped for the quarter-finals where they blitzed Cork. Joe scored 5 points in a 12-point win. Joe put on another great show as they beat Tipperary in the semi-final, scoring 10 points. Galway returned to the All-Ireland final for another crack at Kilkenny.

There was no doubt that Galway and Kilkenny were the two best teams in the country. It was the final everyone wanted to see. Could Galway and Joe Canning finally get over the line? Or would the Cats get the cream once more?

'Lads, we've beaten this lot before. You know you can do it. Keep it tight early. Take your scores and we'll rattle them.'

Joe the Great

Joe was tying up his bootlaces as Anthony Cunningham delivered his speech. Joe didn't need to be pumped up any more. It was the All-Ireland final. Everything was on the line and he couldn't stand the thought of losing again.

As the teams lined up for the anthems, Kilkenny were cool and calm as ever. It seemed that this was what they did every year on the first Sunday in September.

Galway were on top from early on. Johnny Coen led from the back with a great block.

At the other end, Joe got on the scoresheet and Cyril Donnellan picked off a massive score from long range. Despite a goal from Kilkenny's T.J. Reid, Galway went into the break three points ahead. The last score of the first half had been a magic point from Joe.

Over the bar! The men from the west are right in this!

Their lead soon disappeared. It was all Kilkenny as they outscored Galway by nine points to two in the next twenty minutes. It was slipping away from Galway again. Joe

The Cats Again

wasn't at his best, even though he grabbed a late goal from the penalty spot. It wasn't enough.

The Cats are once again the All-Ireland champions!

Galway had to accept defeat once more.

Kilkenny captain Joey Holden climbed the famous Croke Park steps and lifted the Liam MacCarthy Cup. Joe could only watch on. He felt hopeless. He had scored 1-8 but still ended up on the losing side. With every passing year, his dream was slipping away.

With or without King Henry, Kilkenny had proven they were still the greatest. Joe never wanted to see those black and amber stripes again.

Joe finished the season as the top scorer in the championship. He had scored an incredible 5 goals and 55 points. But some people still said he had a bad year!

There was only one way he could keep everyone quiet. He had to finally win the All-Ireland. It became his obsession.

Chapter 20

Home Comforts

Joe was wondering if his time would ever come. Like his brother Ollie, would he always be remembered as one of the greatest players never to win an All-Ireland? Joe was feeling a bit sorry for himself but he was suddenly snapped back to reality. He got some bad news from home.

'Joe, I've something to tell you,' said his mam as he sat in her kitchen having a cup of tea. 'I have cancer.'

Home Comforts

'Oh, Mam. No.' Joe was so upset he could hardly get the words out. He was so close to his mam all his life. Joe loved her so much. He was even named after her. Josephine and Joe. When he was growing up, he went everywhere with her. She always came to his matches. She would stitch holy medals into his shorts to give him luck on the field. She was so proud watching Joe grow up into the great hurler and man he was.

'Don't worry, Joe. I'm going to be fine. I'm starting treatment.'

Joe didn't know what to say. They just had a big hug. Joe was fighting back tears but he wanted to stay strong for his mam.

There was more bad news to come just a few months later. His dad Seán had cancer too. It was hard for Joe and all the family to get their head around it. It made no sense. It seemed so unfair that both his mam and dad could be sick at the same time. Joe was in a spin.

Over the next few months, Joe felt a change inside him. For some reason, all the pressure he felt playing hurling for Galway melted away. He was no longer obsessed with wanting to win. He realised he had been living inside a bubble all this time.

Slowly, he started to change how he thought. He spent more time with his mam and dad as they got treatment and started to get better. He visited home more often. He started to enjoy life a bit more. He realised that hurling wasn't everything.

The family kept the news of their parents' illness to themselves. Nobody really knew apart from their closest friends and relations.

Before long, the doctors told his mam and dad that the treatment had worked and they were better. Everyone was so relieved. They had a holiday in Spain to celebrate.

Joe was ready to go back hurling again. He had a new freshness for the game. From now on, he played hurling for fun. It was just a sport, after all. A hobby. He did it for his mam and dad, nobody else. He wanted to see the smiles on their faces when Galway won. He wanted to make them proud.

Home Comforts

The atmosphere wasn't great in the squad when they came back together. Last year's loss had hurt. The players were sick of near misses and falling short. They had been knocked out of the last four All-Irelands. Were they just unlucky? Or did they need something else? Something to get them over the line when it mattered most?

After lots of hard conversations, the players decided they wanted a change. They wanted a new manager.

It wasn't an easy thing to do. They fought long and hard about it. Many people in Galway and around the country thought it was very unfair on Anthony Cunningham. He had just led them to an All-Ireland final. But the players got their way and Micheál Donoghue came in as the new boss in December 2015. The players had a lot to prove.

A new Galway team started to emerge. They were younger and fresher. Joe was one of the older players now. He had to lead by example.

Joe the Great

One night before training, he addressed the squad. He wanted to lift the pressure from them. He outlined the expectations for the year ahead.

'When you don't win every year, people get fed up. I know the feeling. I've lost more than most. But Galway have only won four All-Irelands ever. Think about it. The last one was a few days before I was born. We shouldn't be expected to win the All-Ireland. Let's embrace it. Let's take it on board. Let's work harder than ever before and let's prove everyone wrong.'

The younger lads looked up to Joe. They would do anything to help him win the All-Ireland he wanted so badly.

The team clicked straight away. They whizzed past Westmeath and then outscored Offaly before another heavy defeat to Kilkenny in the Leinster final. They grew in strength in the knockout stages and beat a good Clare team by two goals. Joe scored 1-8 and was starting to find his feet again. He was enjoying his hurling and life was good.

Home Comforts

Then came Tipperary in the All-Ireland semi-final.

It was a tight, tense game. Joe was in the wars early on and got some treatment for a blood injury. Midway through the first half, disaster struck. He was sprinting for a ball near the Cusack Stand when he felt something rip.

Owwwwwww!

Joe went down holding his leg. The physios knew straight away it was bad but Joe didn't believe them. He wanted to play on but they wouldn't let him. He had to come off and watch from the sidelines as Galway lost the match. Another year down the drain.

When Joe saw the doctor a few days later, he found out how bad his injury was. He had ripped his hamstring from the bone. He had no power in his leg and couldn't sit at all. It was so painful. He had surgery in Cork and was on crutches with his leg in a brace for six weeks.

He faced seven or eight months out of action. But Joe being Joe, he aimed to be back in six.

Chapter 21

UNICEF
A Glimpse of Hope

Joe took some time off over the winter. He had joined the children's charity UNICEF as an ambassador. They invited him to visit the city of Aleppo in Syria. It was a dangerous place to go and his family were worried about his safety.

Joe felt like he needed to do it. A war had been going on for years there and thousands of people had been killed. Many of them were children. Joe wanted to show people what it was like there so they would help.

When he arrived, his eyes were opened to a different world. He was in Zaatari, a refugee camp on the border between Syria and Jordan. Life was difficult there. But Joe quickly noticed that the children still lived with joy.

Joe had seen plenty of suffering in his life. He'd played in some of the toughest matches, battled injuries, and fought through the pain of near-misses with Galway's hurling team. But nothing prepared him for what he saw on his UNICEF trip.

He met children who had lost everything – homes, families and their futures. But they still had hope.

He saw a group of children running and kicking a worn-out ball, their faces lit up with laughter and excitement. Joe walked over and joined in. One of the boys, whose name was Hassan, roared at Joe with pride. 'I'm the best footballer in the camp!'

Joe laughed. 'Are you now?' he said. 'Well, have you ever played hurling?'

Joe the Great

Of course, Joe had brought a hurl and sliotar all the way to Syria. He walked towards the group of children. One of the boys threw a ball over to him, a shy grin on his face. Joe bent down and picked it up, bouncing it lightly in his hands.

'You want to play?' Joe asked.

The child's eyes lit up. 'Yes! Yes, please!' he said, running back to his friends.

As Joe joined in the game, he felt so happy. For a few moments, the world seemed a little bit brighter. The children's laughter rang out. Joe smiled. This was why he did what he did. For a moment the children all forgot where they were and how hard their life was because of the war. That was the magic of sport.

As Joe stood there, he remembered his own childhood in Portumna. He'd spent countless hours on the field, practising hurling with his brothers, dreaming of the day he'd play for Galway. His parents had supported him and helped him through every loss and every win. But these children didn't have that same security. They couldn't play without fear.

UNICEF A Glimpse of Hope

Joe looked around at the camp, seeing rows of tents with families huddled together. It wasn't much, but it was their home, for now. UNICEF was here, giving support. They gave the children a chance to go to school or to see a doctor when they got sick. Joe was happy to do what he could to help. And if that meant helping them forget their worries with a simple game of hurling, that was enough for him.

Joe couldn't help but think back to his own journey with Galway. It hadn't been easy. There had been years of disappointment, of coming so close and falling short. But through all the struggles, there had been one thing that kept him going: the belief that tomorrow would be better. For these children that was not the case. They had lived through the pain of war. And yet they were still laughing, playing and living.

Chapter 22
The Holy Grail

Galway knew they had come close last year. Only for Joe's injury they might have gone all the way. It was their second year under Micheál Donoghue. The young players had a season under their belt. Joe was back fit and firing after a long break over the winter. They set their sights on the All-Ireland. Nothing was going to stop them.

They flew out of the traps, beating Dublin in the Leinster quarter-final in Tullamore. Joe

The Holy Grail

bagged nine points, five of them frees. Then came Offaly, who lost by even more. Galway notched up 33 points to Offaly's 14. Joe added seven more to his tally.

Next up was the Leinster final. Kilkenny had suffered a shock defeat in the semi-final, so for once the final was a different line-up.

Wexford now stood in Galway's way, although not for long. Joe was right on the money again, scoring 10 points in a superb team display. Galway were the Leinster champions and they did it in style. A nine-point win made everyone sit up and take notice. It wasn't just the scores. It was the whole team. They were playing as a unit. Joe was working harder than ever. They were all set up for an almighty semi-final tussle with Tipperary.

Only a point had separated the teams in their last two meetings. There was nothing between them again.

Joe had a terrible start. He struggled to get on the ball. He missed a couple of easy frees and wasted three good chances for goal. It was very unlike him.

'Come on, Joe. Chin up,' roared Burke, trying to snap him out of it.

Joe was furious with himself. But Galway soon steadied the ship. Whelan and Conor Cooney were flying and Tipperary were just a point ahead by half-time.

It was a rip-roaring contest from beginning to end. Both teams were going for it. Suddenly, Joe came alive. He boomed over a massive free to put Galway ahead. But Tipperary's Pádraic Maher matched him all the way. There was nothing between the two teams in the closing stages. It looked to be heading for a draw. Joe was so sick of losing. He wasn't letting this one slip, no matter what.

Four minutes into injury time, Joe launched a free from deep within his own half. It fell short and was quickly cleared by the Tipperary backs. Everyone in the stadium expected the whistle to blow for a draw but Joe chased it down. Johnny Coen picked up the ball way

The Holy Grail

out on the right-hand side, along the touchline near the halfway line. Coen flicked a hand pass to Joe, who was surrounded by three Tipperary players. In an instant, he gathered the sliotar, took a quick glance at the posts and fired a shot.

It was do or die. He watched it like a hawk as it looped high into the Dublin sky. Everyone in the stadium held their breath. The country came to a standstill. It seemed to hang in the air forever. Joe's eyes were bulging as he watched it sail towards the target.

Canning again! It's a miracle shot! Over the bar!

Joe pumped his fist in the air. The Galway fans went wild. The Tipperary players slumped to the ground. Joe had done it. Galway were into the All-Ireland final, where Waterford awaited.

'Yeesss, Joe!' roared Cooney. 'How do you do it?'

'That was a tap-over. It was handy,' joked Burke.

Joe the Great

'I didn't want to lose again, lads. I couldn't face a replay. I was too wrecked!' said Joe with a big grin on his face.

The traffic was savage on the way home. All the Galway fans were singing and beeping their horns as they headed out the road from Dublin. They were on top of the world. But the happiness didn't last too long.

Just a few days later, Galway hurling was shocked again. Word started to spread that Tony Keady, the great player from the eighties, had died peacefully in his sleep. Joe had looked up to Tony so much when he was young. He had visited his workshop every day. Tony had taught Joe so much of what he knew about hurling. He was only 53.

Galway came to a standstill for his funeral. Players from across the country came to pay their respects to one of the all-time greats.

Joe was in the middle of it, trying to figure it all out. Once more, life made no sense. He looked to the heavens and closed his eyes. He thought of all the great fun and mischief he got

The Holy Grail

up to with Tony over the years and he made a promise.

'Tony,' he whispered to himself. 'We're going to win the All-Ireland for you.'

***

Three weeks later, Joe led Galway onto the Croke Park pitch for his fourth All-Ireland final. He had drawn one and lost two before. He had a sense of calm now. Everything was going to be okay.

The noise rose as the crowd of 82,300 fans stood to their feet. The referee picked up the sliotar. Joe tightened the straps of his helmet, gripped his hurley and looked up to the heavens. This was it.

The game was as close as everybody expected it to be. The two best teams in the country both wanted a win so badly.

With 20 minutes left, it was all square. It was now or never. David Burke landed two beauties and Joe stuck over another free.

Joe the Great

'You're flying today,' said Burkey.

'Come on!' Joe roared to the crowd.

With a minute to go, Niall Burke was fouled and Joe stepped up for the free. He took his time to stop and relax. He took a few deep breaths as he stood over the ball. He took aim, fired and split the posts. Right through the middle.

What a score! Does he ever miss? Canning does it again!

Three minutes of stoppage time were added to play but Galway knew it was in the bag. The referee blew the whistle.

Galway are the All-Ireland champions!

Joe turned to face the crowd, raising both his fists in celebration. More than anything else, he felt a sense of relief, just pure emotion. They had finally done it. People young and old were crying in the stands. His mam and dad were somewhere in the crowd too. He eventually found them and they shared big hugs and tears.

'Can you believe it, Mam? We did it!' said Joe.

The Holy Grail

'I'm so proud of you,' she replied as she squeezed him in tight to her.

'I couldn't have done it without you, Mam.'

As Joe made his way back to the dressing room, he took a moment to himself. His dream had finally come true. He thought of his childhood growing up. He thought of running around the house in the helmet and jersey that were too big for him. He remembered the puck-abouts on the farm as he learned from his dad, his sister and brothers. He thought of his mam and dad taking him to training.

He remembered his first real match with the school in Gortanumera. He remembered the day he took the tractor tyres from the silage heap to use as shooting targets. He thought of all the years with Portumna, the Galway minors and under-21s.

He thought of his college years in Limerick and all the good days too. He also thought of the injuries and criticism, when he might have given up, and all the defeats to Kilkenny and King Henry.

Joe the Great

Mostly, Joe thought about those who weren't there to enjoy the day. His old teammate Niall Donohue should have been on the pitch celebrating with them. And Tony Keady, who had died just three weeks before.

A tear came to Joe's eye. He never hurled for himself. He always did it for them.

Chapter 23
The One that Got Away

Joe made sure he enjoyed winning the All-Ireland. He had worked hard enough for it and he knew the chance might never come again. He enjoyed partying and celebrating with his teammates.

But the real joy came on a quiet day back home in Gortanumera when he revisited his old school. So many excited pupils and many of his old teachers were there. He showed them the Liam MacCarthy Cup and his All-Ireland medal. It was a special moment.

Joe the Great

The winter celebrations passed quickly. Soon it was time to focus on hurling again. Joe was hungry for more success, and he started the season on fire. He scored a goal and 12 points in a win over Kilkenny and another 12 against Wexford.

Galway then played out another titanic tussle against Kilkenny in the Leinster final. They drew 18 points each the first day, setting up a replay. Joe fired another ten terrific points, leading the charge for the Tribesmen as they won a classic match at Semple Stadium by 1-28 to 3-15 to win the Leinster title.

***

The All-Ireland series was just as exciting. Galway and Clare played out a pulsating draw in the semi-final. It was hard to believe the final score was 1-30 to 1-30.

In the replay, Joe went up another gear again, scoring eight points to lead Galway to another All-Ireland final. He was on a one-man

The One that Got Away

mission to bring Galway to the top again.

Now they were off to the decider again, this time against Limerick.

The roar of the crowd was deafening as Joe stood in the tunnel of Croke Park, his hurley resting on his shoulder. Once again, a sea of maroon and white flags waved in the stands. The Galway fans were in full voice, their hopes and dreams riding on this team. But across the pitch stood Limerick, a young, fearless squad hungry for their first All-Ireland title in 45 years.

Joe could feel the tension in the air. This wasn't just a match – it was a battle for history.

The whistle blew, and the game sprang to life. Limerick struck first, with Aaron Gillane firing over a point after just two minutes. Joe clenched his jaw, his eyes narrowing as he watched the sliotar sail over the bar. He knew Galway needed to respond quickly.

In the seventh minute, he stepped up for a 65. The crowd held its breath as he steadied himself, his eyes fixed on the posts. With a smooth swing of his hurley, he sent the ball soaring over the bar.

'Yeesss!' he roared as the Galway fans erupted in cheers.

His teammates slapped him on the back. 'Nice one, Joe!' shouted David Burke, the captain and Joe's closest friend on the pitch.

The scores went back and forth, with Joe landing another point to level the game at five points apiece. But Limerick were relentless. A minute later, Graeme Mulcahy scrambled the ball over the line for a goal, giving Limerick a two-point lead. Joe gritted his teeth, his mind racing. He knew they couldn't let Limerick get too far in front.

'Come on, lads!' shouted Joe, his voice cutting through the noise. 'We're still in this. Keep fighting!'

By half-time, Limerick led 1-10 to 0-9, and the Galway dressing room was tense. Manager Micheál Donoghue stood in the centre, his voice calm but firm. 'This is it, lads. This is what champions are made of. We've been here

The One that Got Away

before. We know what it takes. Now go out there and show it.'

Joe sat with his helmet in his hands. 'We're not done yet,' he said, his voice steady. 'We've come too far to let this slip.'

The second half began with Limerick picking up where they left off. Kyle Hayes fired over two quick points, extending their lead to six. Joe tried to rally his team, but Limerick's momentum was building.

Then, in the 54th minute, disaster struck for Galway. A mistake from Gearóid McInerney allowed Tom Morrissey to pounce, firing a low, powerful shot into the net. Limerick were now nine points ahead, and the Galway fans fell silent.

Joe felt a surge of anger, but he refused to let it show. 'Don't let the heads drop, lads!' he shouted. 'We're not finished yet!'

In the first minute of added time, Conor Whelan gave Galway a glimmer of hope, firing a powerful shot to the net.

Gooooooooaaaaaaallllll!

Then deep into stoppage time, Galway got a penalty. Joe stepped up to take it. The pressure was unreal. But he closed his eyes and took a deep breath. Then he stepped up to power the sliotar home.

Goooooooaaaaaaallllllll!

Big Joe ... Back of the net! It's a rocket!

The crowd roared, and the game shifted. The most unlikely comeback was on.

'Come on, boys!' Joe shouted, his voice hoarse with effort. 'We can do this!'

Joe soon added another free. They were just two points behind now. 'That's what we needed!' shouted Johnny Glynn, wrapping an arm around Joe's shoulders.

Galway were surging. A minute later, Niall Burke fired over a point, and the deficit was just one. And right in the last few seconds, they got a chance to level the game.

Galway were awarded a free deep in their own half. It was a difficult chance, but Joe stepped up. He took a moment to compose

The One that Got Away

himself, his eyes fixed on the posts. He struck the ball, but he knew straight away he didn't catch it perfectly. It still had a chance. He watched as it spun towards the posts.

The stadium fell silent for just a second. Time seemed to freeze. Joe's heart was in his mouth. But the ball was slowing down and Galway hearts sank with it, as it dropped short of the posts and Limerick cleared it away.

The final whistle blew, and Limerick were crowned All-Ireland champions. Joe stood on the pitch, his hands on his hips, as the Limerick players celebrated around him. Galway had come so close, but it wasn't to be.

As he made his way off the pitch, Joe was greeted by the Galway fans clapping him, still proud of their team. He waved to the crowd, a small smile breaking through the disappointment. 'We'll be back,' he thought to himself. 'This isn't the end.'

At the end of the season, Joe was named on the All Star team for a fifth time. It was a huge honour and showed he was well on

Joe the Great

his way to becoming an all-time great of the game. But he would swap each of his All Star awards for one more All-Ireland title.

Chapter 24
The Sideline King

The end was nearer than the beginning now for Joe. He still had the hunger for more hurling and he still had the talent and skill. But his body was showing signs of wear and tear. The injuries were starting to take their toll.

The 2019 season was supposed to be a fresh start. After the heartbreak of losing the All-Ireland final to Limerick, Joe was determined to lead Galway back to glory. But life had other plans. In the league semi-final against Waterford he suffered a serious groin injury.

Owwwwwww!

He faced surgery and a long spell on the sidelines.

The recovery process was hard. Joe spent hours in physiotherapy, pushing his body to its limits. He worked tirelessly to regain strength, often staying late at the gym after his sessions were over.

Away from the pitch, he had a bit more time to do other things. He started a restaurant business that kept him busy. He played golf when he could, and he had more time to spend with his girlfriend Meg. They were getting closer and closer and around this time he knew he was going to marry her. But no matter how busy he was, the pull of the game was always there.

'You're mad, Joe,' his brother Ollie joked one evening as they sat in the family kitchen. 'You've been through the wringer, and you're still itching to get back out there.'

The Sideline King

Joe smiled. 'What can I say? Hurling's in my blood.'

By the time Joe returned to action in June, Galway's championship hopes were in danger. They faced Dublin in the final round in Leinster, needing a win to keep their season alive. Joe came on as a substitute, his first appearance since the injury. But it was clear he wasn't at his best. Galway lost and Joe's season was over before it even began.

***

The next season was like no other. The world had been turned upside down by the Covid-19 pandemic, and the GAA championship was no different. Games were played in empty, silent stadiums.

Galway began in October with a Leinster championship clash against Wexford. It was strange to have no fans in Croke Park. The usual roar was replaced by the sound of hurleys striking sliotars and the shouts of players.

Joe the Great

But Joe was in his element. From the first whistle, he was everywhere, pulling the strings and landing scores from all over the field. He finished the game with nine points, including two stunning sideline cuts. Galway cruised to a 1-27 to 0-17 victory.

But the real test came in the Leinster final against Kilkenny. It was always tough against the Cats. Joe fought hard, scoring 14 points, but Galway couldn't break through Kilkenny's defence. The final whistle blew, and Galway's dreams of a Leinster title were dashed.

The All-Ireland series brought a chance to make up for the disappointment. Galway's first test was a quarter-final clash against Tipperary, the defending champions. The match was a classic. Joe had a day to remember, scoring an incredible 14 points. He landed twelve frees and two more trademark sideline cuts.

Tipperary's sharpshooters were in fine form too. But Joe's leadership kept Galway in the hunt. With the scores level in the dying moments, Joe stepped up for a crucial free.

The Sideline King

The stadium, empty though it was, felt like it was holding its breath. He took his time, steadied himself, and sent the sliotar soaring over the bar.

He's done it! Joe the Great strikes again!

Galway held on to win 3-23 to 2-24.

Joe's teammates mobbed him. 'You were unbelievable out there,' roared David Burke.

'You weren't so bad yourself Burkey,' said Joe as the pair hugged.

The win set up an All-Ireland semi-final clash against Limerick, the team that had broken Galway's hearts in the 2018 final. It was a match that would go down in history, not just for the result, but for Joe's incredible performance.

From the first whistle, Joe covered every blade of grass. He dropped deep to make the play, set up his teammates with pinpoint passes, and scored freely from all angles. But it was his sideline cuts that stole the show. Time and time again, he stepped up to take

Joe the Great

the difficult shots. And time and time again, he delivered. By the end of the match, he had scored four points from sideline cuts – a new championship record.

The Limerick defenders could only watch in awe as he split the posts from impossible angles. 'That's unreal, Joe!' shouted Conor Whelan, his voice filled with awe.

But despite Joe's heroics, Galway fell short. Limerick's firepower proved too much, and they won by 0-27 to 0-24. As the final whistle blew, Joe fell to his knees. He had given everything, but it wasn't enough.

Chapter 25
The Final Whistle

Joe began the next year with hope. But soon everything changed. It was his 14th season with Galway and likely to be his last. He knew the journey was coming to an end.

Galway were determined to bounce back from all the disappointments of previous years. But that hope soon turned to sadness. Joe got the sad news that his mam Josephine's cancer had come back. This time it didn't look good. It was a tough time for all the family, especially

Joe. But hurling was the only way he knew to keep his mind off things.

The championship began. It was a relief for Joe to get back on the pitch and do what he did best. And in July, in the All-Ireland qualifiers against Waterford, he achieved a historic milestone. Joe scored nine points in the match to become the top scorer in the history of the hurling championship. The magic moment came just past the hour mark.

Canning steps inside with all his pace and power ... flicks his wrist and it flies just over the bar ... A point for Galway and a moment of history for the Portumna man!

'Yes, Joe!' roared David Burke as the ball sailed over. 'You've made history!' He was so proud.

The crowd stood to their feet in applause. Joe had overtaken the great Henry Shefflin as the all-time top scorer, finishing with a remarkable total of 27 goals and 486 points. The prince had finally outgrown the king.

The Final Whistle

But the moment was bittersweet. Despite Joe's heroics, Galway fell short, losing by a narrow margin. They were out of the championship again and Joe knew straight away that this would be his last moment on a hurling field with Galway.

He met his dad and brother Ivan on the pitch.

'That's it. That's me finished!' said Joe to his dad.

His dad didn't say anything. But Ivan piped up in shock. 'What are you on about? Will you stop!' he said with disbelief on his face.

Joe spoke on the phone to his mam. She told him not to make any decision right there and then. To take some time. But Joe had made up his mind.

In the dressing room, he told his teammates that he was calling it a day. This was the last time he would share the special bond of the dressing room with them.

'It's been an incredible journey,' said Joe. 'I've been lucky to wear the Galway jersey for

Joe the Great

so many years, to play alongside some of the greatest hurlers of all time, and to represent my county with pride. But now it's time to step away. I'll always be grateful for the memories and the friendships I've made along the way.'

His teammates gave him a big clap and there was huge sadness in the room. There would be no more high balls caught, no more pinpoint frees or net-bursting goals. No more shuddering shoulders or tough tackles. No more trademark sideline cuts. Joe the Great was stepping away. This was the last time anyone would see one of the legends of the game in action.

***

Joe sat on a bench in his local church in Portumna, holding a sliotar in one hand. He wasn't here for a match or to talk about hurling. He was here to talk to his mam, even though she wasn't there in person. Her grave was just outside, under the shade of a tall tree. But Joe felt her everywhere.

The Final Whistle

She had died in the winter and now he missed her every day. But sometimes he felt like she was still with him. Joe's mam had been the kind of person who didn't want others to worry about her. Even when she was sick, she'd smile and say, 'I'm fine, love. Don't be fussing over me.' But Joe had known deep down that things weren't fine.

Joe had learned a lot from his mam. She had taught him to stay calm under pressure and to always think of the people around him. 'A hurler isn't just playing for themselves,' she used to say. 'You're playing for the whole parish, for the people in the stands, for everyone who's ever picked up a hurl in Portumna.'

Losing his mam was the hardest thing Joe had ever faced. He remembered the last days in the hospital, bringing her Calippo ice pops because she liked the cold feeling on her tongue.

He walked out to her grave and took a few Ferrero Rocher chocolates from his pocket — her favourite. He left one on the headstone

Joe the Great

and ate one himself, smiling at the memory of her laughter. 'She loved these,' he said to himself quietly.

***

Later that year Joe and his girlfriend Meg got married. It was a beautiful ceremony in Monaleen Church in County Limerick. All their family and friends were there. It was a memorable day.

During the mass came a special moment. A butterfly flew around the altar. Joe watched as it fluttered its wings and eventually rested on the altar. He felt it was a sign that his mam Josephine was with him on the day.

The day passed in a whirlwind of music, dancing and heartfelt speeches. Joe's best man told stories from their childhood, while Meg's family spoke about her kindness, strength and the love she and Joe shared.

They stepped onto the dance floor for their first dance together as a married couple. Their

The Final Whistle

family and friends watched, laughing and cheering. Joe thought how lucky he was.

Sometime later, Meg told Joe some happy news. She was pregnant with their first baby. Joe was overjoyed.

The next year, Meg gave birth to a beautiful baby girl. To Joe, she was flawless. It was the happiest day of his life. And he knew exactly what name he wanted to give her. Josie, after his mam. Josephine, Joe and Josie. It was perfect. A butterfly flew past the window and settled on a flower outside. Joe smiled.

His mind wandered back over his own life. It seemed like only yesterday he was a child himself, dreaming of growing up to be an All Star hurler. He remembered his first days in school in Gortanumera, his early days playing hurling and all the fun he had at home with his family. It seemed to pass in the blink of an eye.

He thought of all the days in the Galway shirt. The blood, sweat and tears. The big wins, the championship trophies, the points and goals scored, the All Star awards. And,

Joe the Great

most of all, that glorious September when Galway finally won the All-Ireland.

He looked down at baby Josie sleeping in his arms, with his wife Meg beside him. His days playing hurling with Galway were over. They were a memory now. But he was happy. He had everything he ever wanted in life. All his dreams had come true. He would forever be Joe the Great.